Advanced Bass Tackle and Boats

Books by A. D. Livingston

Advanced Bass Tackle and Boats

by A. D. Livingston

J. B. Lippincott Company
Philadelphia and New York

Grateful acknowledgment is made to the following for permission to reprint the quotations used in this book:

BASSMASTER Magazine, published by the Bass Anglers Sportsman Society, Montgomery, Alabama 36109, for the passage on pages 196–97.

Dodd, Mead & Company, for the paragraph on page 28 from *Lucas on Bass Fishing* by Jason Lucas.

Gudebrod Brothers Silk Company, Inc., for the passage on pages 77–80.

Lowrance Electronics, Inc., for the passage on pages 110–11.

Ray Jefferson, Ideas, Inc., for the passages on pages 112–13 and 135–38.

Ray-O-Vac Division, ESB Incorporated, for the passage on page 151.

Winchester Press, for the passage on pages 37–39 from *Fiberglass Rod Making* by Dale P. Clemens.

U. S. LIBRARY OF CONGRESS CATALOGING IN PUBLICATION DATA

Livingston, A   D   birth date
Advanced bass tackle and boats.

Includes index
1. Black bass fishing.   2. Fishing tackle.
3. Fishing boats.   I. Title.
SH681.L53   799.1'7'58   75–15557
ISBN–0–397–01100–8

For Ike

Contents

Preface

WHENEVER TWO BASS ANGLERS get together for any length of time, the conversation won't merely drift toward tackle and gear. They'll be hot onto the subject within two minutes! Because I've never seen a bassman who wasn't interested in tackle, I reasoned that they might also like to read about it. As far as I know, there has never been a book like *Advanced Bass Tackle and Boats*. Yet I feel that such a book is needed, and needed now, because millions of anglers are pursuing bass fishing more and more zealously—and because of the diversity and the complexity and the sheer bulk of bassing gear that has been put on the market during the past few years. We now have all sorts of transistorized electronic gear, including underwater light intensity meters, sonar devices, surface and subsurface temperature indicators, and even oxygen monitors. The specialized fishing machine known as the bass boat. Hot new lures. Improved lines. Highly engineered reels. Rods made of space-age fibers and fittings. And so on. It's fantastic, and the modern bassman has for his pleasure fishing aids undreamed of in old Izaak Walton's philosophy.

I have done a lot of research for this book, and I believe it will be

9

valuable to any bass angler—newcomer or pro. I wrote the book to be read chapter by chapter, but I also set it up as a reference work. The text is indexed for quick use, and Part Four contains by far the most complete (and annotated) list of tackle and bass boat manufacturers ever compiled. Much of the research was done on a "rush" basis in an attempt to gather up-to-the-minute information on all the bassing gear on the market. Although this sort of research was necessary, I feel that my lifelong appreciation of quality tackle, together with some disgruntling experiences with junk, enabled me to *talk* about tackle and gear instead of merely cataloging what's available. I have tried to be objective without entirely killing the vigor of my opinions. If I seem enthusiastic about a particular item, it is because I believe in it—not because I work for the manufacturer or own stock in the firm. Unlike some outdoor writers, I have no interest whatsoever in any tackle company.

Good fishing. Keep your hook sharp, your line tight, and your transducer clean.

A. D. LIVINGSTON

Illustration Credits

The photographs and drawings on the following pages are reproduced through the courtesy of the sources listed below. (All photographs not otherwise attributed are by the author.)

Pages 26, 69, 86, 96, 189, and 200 (by Phillip Seifert): Louisiana Tourist Development Commission.

Page 46, top: Pfleuger Sporting Goods Division; bottom: Garcia Corporation.

Page 58: Gladding Corporation.

Page 59: Browning Arms Company.

Page 79 (drawing): Gudebrod Brothers Silk Company, Inc.

Pages 108 and 130: Tennessee Valley Authority.

Pages 110 and 134 (photographs) and pages 136 and 137 (drawings): Ray Jefferson.

Pages 113, 123, and 129: Lowrance Electronics, Inc.

Page 114: Southeastern Marine Supply, Inc.

Page 117 (drawing): Telisons International Corporation.

Pages 124, 165, and 192: Ouachita Marine and Industrial Corporation.

Pages 125, 129, and 131: Fishmaster Products, Inc.

Page 150 (by Joel Arrington): North Carolina Travel and Promotion
  Division.
Page 156: Bass Anglers Sportsman Society.
Page 160: Glastron Boat Company.
Pages 161 and 167: Ranger Boats.
Page 164: Mercury Marine.
Page 171: Johnson Outboards.
Pages 179 and 188: Evinrude Motors.
Page 184: Johnny Reb Lure Company.
Page 201: Florida News Bureau.
Page 203: Texas Tourist Development Agency.
Page 204: South Dakota Department of Game, Fish, and Parks.

Part One
Tackle and Gear

1

Rod Fittings and Handles

NOT LONG AGO, I renewed my fishing acquaintance with a man who had been one of my boyhood heroes, a real bass angler who had a bait-casting outfit and dozens of lures and even a boat. But either I have become too much of a stickler about my gear or he has become downright sloppy about his. Frankly, the condition of his two rods shocked me. The tips were not only grooved from repeated use but were also pitted and corroded. It probably never occurred to him that his rod tips and guides were abrading his line, so that some of the bass that got away weren't necessarily all that big.

Most savvy bass fishermen know that tips and guides are important, but I doubt that one in a hundred realizes just how important. The average bass angler of today makes three times as many casts as he did 20 years ago, largely because the bow-mounted electric motor and other fishing aids permit him to use his time casting instead of keeping the boat in position with paddle or oars. Recently I read that the typical bassman makes 2,000 casts per day. If each cast averages only 40 feet out and 40 feet back in, 160,000 feet of line pass back and forth through the guides and tip. That's 30 miles. I might add that many anglers, especially the bass pros, will average more than 2,000 casts per day. Much more. Some tournament fishermen make up to 10 casts per minute, depending on the lure they are using.

Although there have been some recent innovations in guide and tip design, the most important consideration is the material from which they are made. Here's my breakdown:

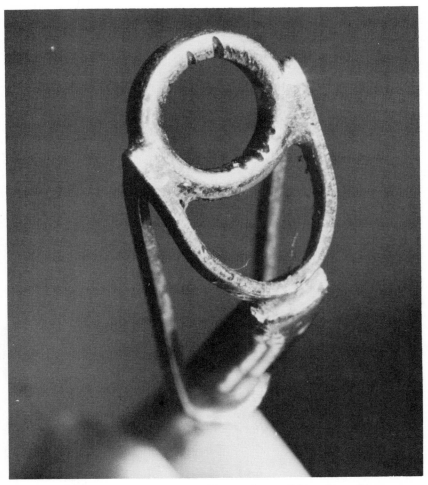

Worm rod guides and tips can quickly weaken a fishing line. The grooves in this rod tip were actually made by monofilament.

Agate. A few years back, agate was considered by some anglers to be the ultimate guide material. A microcrystalline form of quartz, agate is extremely hard; but it is also quite brittle, and is likely to shatter if subjected to hard knocks. It can also chip or form hairline cracks, either of which can ruin even the best fishing line fast.

Another disadvantage of agate guides is that they are comparatively expensive, not only because of the material itself but because of the amount of grinding and polishing required to produce a guide ring. But a few agate fittings are still used on some modern rods. Garcia, for example, features them on a 7-foot heavy-action spinning rod in their Deluxe line. Garcia also markets sets of agate guides for freshwater and saltwater spinning rods.

Stainless steel. A good many of the less expensive rods have guides and tips made of stainless steel. They may be adequate for live bait fishing or other forms of "still" fishing, but they simply don't hold up for casting artificial baits. Although stainless steel can be polished quite smooth and seems to be very hard, monofilament line will wear grooves in it. But a good deal depends on the quality of the guides, and some serious bassmen prefer good stainless steel.

Chromium plate. The better grades of chromium-plated stainless steel guides and tips are a good deal harder than uncoated stainless steel. Chromium itself is hard stuff, and, by some quirk of metallurgy, it is even harder when coated onto another metal in thin layers. Chromium-plated stainless steel guides are lighter than agate (or tungsten carbide) and not as brittle, which means that they can be kicked around more. In my opinion, however, chromium is not quite hard enough for tips on bass fishing rods, although it is probably adequate for guide rings.

Tungsten carbide. During recent years, many of the better fishing rods have been fitted with tungsten carbide guides and tips; rather, with guides and tips having tungsten carbide rings. Typically, a tungsten carbide ring is silver soldered or brazed to a frame of stainless steel or other metal. For many years tungsten carbide was my favorite guide and tip material, but I'm beginning to have my doubts about it. Although it is very hard, it does have some disadvantages. It is brittle, and will shatter from a hard knock or—worse—will sometimes form a hairline crack that can severely abrade a fishing line in short order. Tungsten carbide is heavy, so heavy that it is simply not suitable for guides on ultralight spinning rods and light casting rods. Quite often, however, tungsten carbide tips will be used with chromium-plated stainless steel guides, an arrangement that works very well because the tips are more subject to wear.

Although tungsten carbide does not groove as badly as softer metal, it will eventually become rather grainy and rough. I've heard that cobalt in the metal will corrode away, leaving a coarse edge. I don't have any scientific data, but my experience indicates that carbide tips do, in time, overly abrade fishing lines. My conclusion is that it may be better to have a smoothly grooved tip than a rough nongrooved tip! But the question is purely academic as far as my personal fishing is concerned; I have become devoted to a new guide and tip material, which is discussed next.

Aluminum oxide. For over a year now I've been using a baitcasting rod with Fuji Hard Speed Rings. I fish almost every day and have therefore given the Speed Rings a thorough workout. I have, in fact, run at least 5,000 miles of line back and forth through the Fuji tips and guides, and my 8X lupe shows no wear, no grooves, no rough surface, and no hairline cracks. More important, my line lasts longer, I've broken off fewer lures on snags, and I have lost no lunker bass because of line failure. My conclusion is that the Fuji guides are made of good stuff.

Although aluminum oxide occurs in nature (ruby, in fact, is a form of aluminum oxide), the material in the Fuji guides and tips is a formula used in spacecraft to help withstand the heat of reentry. The Speed Rings are manufactured in Japan by Fuji Kogmo Limited of Shizuok and are distributed in the United States by Lew Childre & Son. Reportedly, Rintaro Ohmura, president of Fuji, developed the guides and used them to win the Japanese surf casting championship. The smoothness and frictionless qualities of the guides permit more distance (up to 20 percent) on the cast. Reduced friction also reduces the chances of backlash, and of course saves wear and tear on the fishing line.

The first step in making the guides and tips is to form the aluminum oxide into rings. These rings are diamond polished and set into a plastic "shock sleeve." Then the ring-and-sleeve units are set in a one-piece stainless frame. The frames are then attached to the rod.

When set in the plastic shock rings and the metal frame, the guides and tip rings are more or less immune to shattering from hard knocks. (I did, however, bend a frame, but it was easily restored to its original shape with no apparent damage.) Although the design of the guides and the construction of the frames seems to be very good, it is the

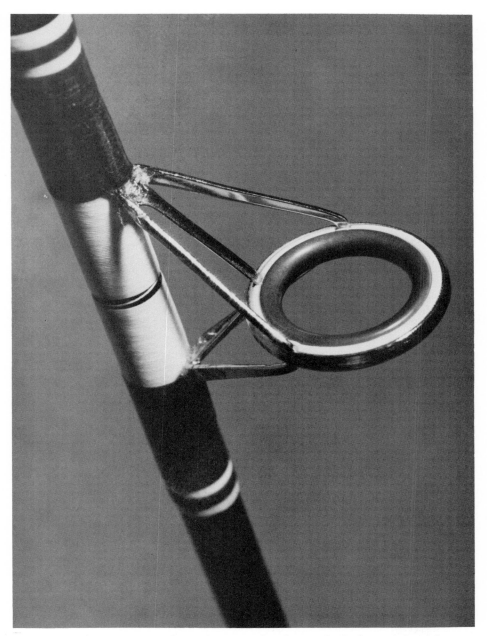

A typical aluminum oxide guide. Note the plastic shock sleeve (white) between the aluminum oxide ring and the outer stainless steel frame.

properties of the aluminum oxide itself that interest me. As proof of hardness, many writers have reported that they filed on the rings for several minutes and couldn't make a scratch. It's true. I tried it myself. Aluminum oxide is somewhat brittle—but not nearly as brittle as tungsten carbide or agate. It is also a good deal lighter than other guide materials. In short, aluminum oxide may not be the best possible guide material, but it's the best I've ever used.

Some of the custom rod makers prefer aluminum oxide, and many rod manufacturers are now using aluminum oxide guides by arrangement with Lew Childre. It is becoming difficult, however, to tell for sure what's a Fuji guide and what's not, and a lot of people are confused about whether guides on a particular rod are aluminum oxide or some other new material. Fenwick calls them "ceramic" guides. Daiwa calls them Dialoy. Bassmaster Pro Shop, which sells the Ray Scott line of rods, calls them space-age speed guides and tips. Zebco calls them Slipstream aluminum oxide.

I wrote a batch of letters to various rod makers, and most of them were reluctant to say that they used Fuji guides. One reputable firm said their guides are "the same as" the Fuji guides. Another said the construction and materials on their guides are "identical to that" of Fuji Speed Rings. A few firms, such as St. Croix, state flatly that they use Fuji guides and tips. As far as I can tell, all of them are either Fuji guides or else they are made from Fuji materials. With one exception.

The new Sintox guides and tips are being manufactured in England. I understand that Gene Bullard Custom Rods had the American franchise but turned it over to Featherweight Products. The first production batch went to Heddon, but the guides are now available to individuals. I have wrapped a set of Sintox guides onto a worm rod, and they work very well. Although the rings are made of aluminum oxide, the construction and design are somewhat different. For one thing, the rings are larger and heavier. For another, no shock sleeve is used. The frame is also heavier and is made from wire instead of stamped metal. I don't object to the absence of plastic shock sleeves if, as the company says, they aren't really needed with the Sintox construction and design. I do, however, believe that the Sintox guides are too heavy for use on ultralight rods. Whether they are as good as, or better, than Fuji guides for heavier rods, only time will tell.

Titanium dioxide. After I had written the aluminum oxide text above, Allan Manufacturing Company introduced their new CerAllan line of titanium dioxide guides and tips. While admitting that the new guide material is softer than aluminum oxide and that it might in time show slight signs of use, the firm believes that titanium dioxide is better than aluminum oxide in prolonging line life. A spokesman for the firm wrote me a convincing letter on this point, but he didn't say anything about how titanium dioxide compares with aluminum oxide on other counts, such as brittleness and weight. Whether titanium dioxide proves to be a better guide material than aluminum oxide is a question that I can't yet answer. I was, however, favorably impressed with a couple of samples Allan sent to me. They seem to be as smooth as the Fuji and Sintox guides, and I'm certain that they will cast satisfactorily. How well they resist wear under hard use remains to be seen.

Most guides and tips are constructed of two major components: the ring and the frame. The exceptions are the snake guides used on fly rods and the "ring" guides made from a single strand of wire (such as the Aetna Foulproof design). The one-piece wire guides have advantages, but the big disadvantage is that the frame and the line "ring" must be made of the same material. On other guides, the frame and the rings can easily be made from different materials, but they must be joined together. In most cases, the construction is adequate, but from time to time I have had rings separate from the frames at the soldered joints.

The only radical construction change in recent years came with the Fuji guides. In addition to a plastic shock sleeve installed between the guide ring and the metal, the entire frame is made in one piece. The aluminum oxide ring and the shock sleeve are fitted into the frame under pressure. I haven't deliberately tried to damage any of the guides on my rods, but one reporter said that he couldn't tear one up by hand, although he was able to force the ring out by using tools. On the other hand, my six-year-old son did somehow manage to pop a ring out while fishing with one of my rods. I carefully squeezed the ring back in place with pliers, and have had no further trouble with it.

Anyhow, here are a few other guide and tip design considerations:

Flex. Ideally, a rod guide should be flexible enough to bend with the rod. On the other hand, the rod guide should be strong enough to resist the bumps and knocks a rod often receives during a hard day's fishing.

The flex problem is usually more important with spinning than with baitcasting rods, simply because the spinning guides are larger and have longer feet. On either casting or spinning rods, as well as on fly rods, flex is more important on ultralight, limber rods than on more rigid sticks. Flex is of virtually no importance on worm rods.

I'm sure that most manufacturers consider flex when designing rod guides, but as far as I know only Gudebrod makes an issue of it. Their Aetna guides, made from a single strand of hard-chromed monel wire, are designed to flex with the rod, thereby eliminating dead spots. The Aetna guides are also light in weight, and are my personal choice for ultralight spinning rods provided that the rod is fitted with an aluminum oxide tip.

Shape. The circle is the traditional shape of guide and tip rings, and it is probably the only shape that will ever be widely used on casting rods.

Recently, however, the Quick people started putting three-sided Polygon guides on their better spinning rods. According to the firm, the line touches these guides at only three points, instead of 360 degrees with circular guides, thereby eliminating friction. On the other hand, the Allan people have started marketing an Ovallan guide, which is, of course, oval in shape. Their idea is that the "wear area" on an oval guide ring is five times larger than on a regular circular guide ring. Thus, there is less chance that the wear area will become grooved. There's something to both points of view, but I'll stick with a regular circular design until Fuji, Sintox, or somebody comes out with oval or polygon rings made from aluminum oxide!

Height and size. On baitcasting rods, the height of the guides is such that the line comes off the reel spool and travels toward the tip in a straight line. Casting rod guides have become pretty much standard, and most anglers (and manufacturers) don't seem to consider the height of their guides. To my knowledge, Fenwick is the only manufacturer in recent years to deviate from standard heights. On their 1400 series Lunkerstiks, Fenwick used a higher guide because, they said, it reduces line slap.

Spinning rods have large, high guides on the butt portion of the rod. The reason for the large rings is that the line comes off the spinning reel in coils and must be funneled toward the tip. Because the sheer weight of large guide rings creates a problem with light spinning rods, I would like to point out that the height of the butt guide is probably more important than the size of the ring. Some butt guides are, in fact, now being made with small rings set in high, fold-down frames. But I doubt that this will catch on in a big way—tiny rings on the butt of a spinning rod just don't *look* right.

*   *   *

One function of guides is to distribute stress properly along a rod blank. When a rod bends from pressure on the line, the stress on any one segment between two guides is greatest at midpoint. The greater the distance between guides, the greater the stress. By the same token, the more guides on a rod (if they are properly spaced), the less the stress at any one point. Strictly from the viewpoint of strength, it would be better to have 50 guides than 5. But this would be impractical not only because of the added weight but also because of the labor required to wrap all those guides. As a practical compromise, the guides on a rod are usually limited from 4 to 6, depending on the length of the blank.

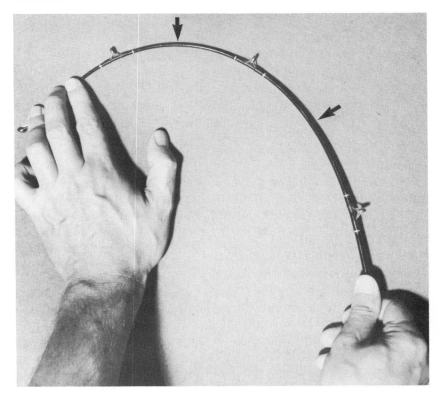

One function of rod guides is to distribute the load evenly. Points of maximum stress are indicated by the arrows. The more properly the guides are spaced on a rod, the less stress there will be at any one point.

On all but the cheapest rods, guides are not equidistant from each other. Instead, they are placed progressively closer together from butt to tip because the rod blank is smaller and more vulnerable at the tip portion. Still another reason for progressive placement is to help keep the line from slapping the rod during the cast. Rod slap not only reduces distance but also makes casting less accurate. In extreme cases, it can even cause backlash.

Fortunately, the spacing of rod guides has been pretty well worked out, and the average angler need not be too concerned about it if he buys a good rod. It is possible to put guides on a rod by trial and error, but the rank amateur at rod making will do well to follow established placement guides for a particular blank's length. Reed Tackle and other firms that sell rod-building materials provide distance tables or patterns with their blanks. On the other hand, each rod blank is different, and an expert rod maker can often improve on factory placement and placement patterns.

Most guides are wrapped to the rod with thread. This is a rather tedious process, and it accounts for a good part of the price of a rod. The quality of workmanship, the number of guides, and the guide ring material go a long way toward establishing a rod's price. Indeed, an expensive rod and a moderately priced rod may well have the same blank, with the price increase incurred solely because of the cost of hardware and workmanship.

As already indicated, the main quality to look for in a guide, and especially in a tip, is a smooth, hard, long-wearing ring surface. The smoother the guide rings, the less friction created on the cast, during the retrieve, and while fighting a fish. But any guide or tip will wear a line to a certain degree. Consequently, it is important that the angler inspect his line frequently. By the same token, any line, and especially monofilament, will wear a guide or tip to one degree or another. Consequently, it is important that the angler frequently inspect or periodically replace his guides and tips.

Worn stainless steel guide rings will show visible evidence of grooving, but tungsten carbide rings aren't as likely to groove out. They may wear or corrode on an almost microscopic basis, so that inspection with the naked eye will not be sufficient. The best bet with tungsten carbide is to replace tips about once a year and guides about once every two years. This is just a rule of thumb, and the angler who fishes quite frequently might want to replace guides and tips more often.

I'm not sure, but the microscopic roughness associated with tungsten carbide rings *may* be more of a function of time and exposure than of the amount of line hauled over them.

The aluminum oxide guides are so new that I don't believe anyone knows, even as a rule of thumb, how often they should be replaced. I do know that they hold up very well under long, hard use and seem to be immune to both frictional wear and corrosion. Whatever time may prove, I plan to keep a close check on my aluminum oxide rings, and I think I'll replace the tips every couple of years, whether or not they need it.

Whatever guides one has on his fishing rods, I want to point out that most anglers who use artificial baits can drastically reduce the wear on guide rings and tips. The trick is to point the rod toward the lure on the retrieve. This is especially important with crank baits, spinnerbaits with large blades, and other lures that "pull" quite a lot. Sometimes it is desirable to impart lure action by twitching the rod tip, and sometimes it is desirable to hold the rod high, as when buzzing a lure across the surface. Still, many anglers would profit by making a conscious effort at pointing the rod tip toward the lure during a straight retrieve. Just remember that the higher the rod tip, the greater the friction created as the line goes over the guide and tip rings.

Remember also that keeping the rod low increases the angler's chances of setting the hook when a strike occurs, because the rod tip makes a longer arc when the angler strikes back. The more limber the rod and the more stretchy the line, the more important it becomes to keep the rod tip low during the retrieve. I don't have any notes to draw from, but my guess is that the average angler holds his rod tip at an angle of about 45 degrees. This is, in my opinion, *the* most common and costly error that an angler makes.

Until recently, cork has been used almost exclusively on all types of fishing rod handles except for the hardwood handles on some saltwater rods. Although cork is made up of air-filled cells, it is a tough, wear-resistant material and is almost impervious to most liquids. The surface of cut cork is made up of microscopic half-spheres, which act like suction cups. This nonslip effect, combined with light weight, makes cork a highly desirable material for rod handle grips.

Dirty cork, however, loses some of its nonslip properties, so that rod handles should be scrubbed with soap and water from time to time.

Holding the rod tip low when retrieving a lure will reduce the wear on rod tips and will also improve the angler's chances of setting the hook. Holding the rod tips high on the retrieve is probably the biggest single mistake that most anglers make.

Fine steel wool does a good job. It is not too unusual for an angler to lose his grip and throw a baitcasting or spincast rod into the water. Cleaning cork handles will give the angler a better hold, and will also make the handle feel more snug and comfortable.

Several grades of cork are used in fishing rod handles. One defect in cork is that it has unidirectional pits running through it. Generally, the fewer the pits, the better the grade of the cork. Most of the top-quality rod handle grips are made with rings of specie cork, in which the pits run in the same direction as the rod blank; this helps prevent water from soaking through the pits and loosening the glue that binds the rings to the handle.

Although cork grips are still used on the majority of fishing rods, some of the newer rods are now being made with grips of more spongy materials. Featherweight Products, for example, markets a baitcasting handle with a contour grip made of molded Kraton. Featherweight also offers Hypalon sleeves for making custom grips. According to the firm, Hypalon is a tough, resilient material that doesn't slip. I haven't made a survey of all the spongy materials being used on rods these days, but a quick check down the rod racks of several tackle shops indicates that such material is becoming quite popular. These new grips are attractive and comfortable, but I have no way of knowing whether they will outlast cork.

At the other extreme, more hardwoods are being used on rod handles. Cordell Tackle offers their Lightnin' Rods with either cork grips or beautiful walnut pistol grips. The firm also sells the walnut handles separately. Garcia offers contoured hardwood grips on several spincast and baitcasting rods in their Deluxe Series, and Lew Childre offers a two-handed hardwood handle for the Speed Sticks. A few other firms also offer similar grips, but wood is still the exception and always will be.

Regardless of whatever kind of material a handle grip is made from, I personally prefer the contour design. If the contour is right for the angler's hand, it makes casting and fishing more comfortable and reduces the chances of throwing rod and reel into the water. If I am using a regular (noncontour) handle, I prefer to have a large butt cap on it. Rubber and plastic slip-on butt caps are available, but sometimes it is difficult to find one to fit certain rod handles. I bought a butt cap to put on an old rod of mine, but it wouldn't stay on even with the help of the glue that was provided with it. Anyone who has trouble finding a suitable butt cap for a particular rod might want to try the rubber or plastic caps made to slip over furniture legs.

Butt caps aren't of much value on most spinning rods because the angler includes the reel's foot in the grip, which makes it highly unlikely that he will lose his hold on the rig. Some anglers prefer very long spinning rod handles and brace them against their belly, so a butt cap may make the rod more comfortable. The trend in light one-hand spinning rigs, however, seems to be toward short handles with the reel seat well back toward the butt, in which case a cap is useless and might even be undesirable.

While spinning rod handles are getting shorter, long handles designed for two-handed casting are becoming more popular on baitcasting rods. I personally don't care for them simply because I prefer to cast with one hand, and a handle over 5 inches long just gets in the way and throws the rod off balance for me. But anglers who fish with long, very stiff blanks may prefer two-handed casting. It really takes two hands to load some of those ultrastiff worm rods for the cast! Anyhow, anyone who wants to try two-handed casting need not necessarily purchase a whole new rod. Featherweight Products markets a baitcasting handle with an 8-inch cork grip, and another with a 12-inch grip. Reed Tackle now offers an extension grip for their all-angle casting handle. Both the Featherweight and the Reed handles have adjustable chucks, so that a wide range of rod blanks can be used with them.

There is a good deal of confusion about whether casting rod handles are straight or offset, and what some books and manufacturers call a straight handle is called an offset handle by other books and manufacturers. The confusion comes about because some sources refer to a sunken reel seat when they specify an offset handle, while others refer to a handle with the grip portion bent slightly downward. As *I* see it, there are three basic types of handles:

Straight. A straight handle is just that. The reel seat is right on top of the handle instead of being sunken. For a while, this was the design standard, but over the past 25 years or so they have all but disappeared, except on saltwater popping rods. But a few straight rod handles are still used on freshwater rods.

Offset. Casting rod handles with sunken, or offset, reel seats are much more popular today than straight handles. Offset handles are easier to use because the reel spool is lowered, and a lower reel spool is easier to thumb—at least to this angler. But many experts in the past have preferred the straight handles. Here are a few words on the subject from Jason Lucas's classic book *Lucas on Bass Fishing*:

> Of late years, about all casting rods except bamboos are made with sunken reel seats; most fishermen have come to regard these as standard. However, a great many expert anglers and tournament casters prefer the straight reel seat and handle, believing that better casting can be done with them. I admit that I am among these, but I suspect that it is only because I learned casting with the high reel seat and am more accustomed to it. I believe that I should like the sunken reel seat better but that all reels are now made with a very low rear pillar; when my thumb is braced upon this, its tip jabs somewhat into the rear of the spool, instead of rocking down more gently on the top, to permit more delicate thumbing.

As Lucas suggested, a good deal depends on habit, and I, for one, learned to cast with an offset handle, have always used one, and probably always will. I find the straight handle awkward to use and ill-fitting. As I see it, one advantage of an offset handle is that it lowers the reel spool and thereby brings the off-coming line down more parallel to the rod and more aligned with the guides and tip.

Offset decurved. Many rods have handles with decurved grips (often called offset), and some handles are available with adjustable grip angles. Decurved handles are almost always used with push-button spincast reels, and they are being used more and more with baitcasting reels. I prefer a "straight" offset handle for baitcasting reels, but this may be a matter of habit. The main thing is that the rod handle feel right in the angler's hand.

Most spinning rods these days come with metal reel seats. The better ones on freshwater rods are usually made with anodized aluminum alloy, and the reel is locked in by two knurled rings threaded to traverse a short portion of the handle. Most of these seats work satisfactorily, and the main thing to look for is comfort. Frankly, most spinning rod seats cramp my hand after half a day of hard fishing.

Incidentally, one of the most comfortable spinning rods I've ever put a grip on is the Quick Super Finessa with a Neo-grip handle. According to the firm, "Soft neoprene rubber, molded to fit your hand, completely encloses the reel seat—eliminates gripping the metal threads and uncomfortable reel seats." I think they've got something, and I noticed that one of the Ray Scott rods uses the same design. On the other hand, I have merely swished one of these rods around in a tackle shop and haven't put it to an all-day test.

Ultralight spinning rods are often equipped merely with two swaged (or sometimes tapered) rings which slide up and down the cork grip. The reel is held in place simply by wedging the rings over the feet of the reel. The disadvantage of this design is that the rings work loose from time to time. One big advantage is that the rings and reel can be moved up or down the rod, allowing the angler to balance the rod the way he wants it. Another advantage is that the rings make for a comfortable grip. I like the simplicity and lightness of rings, especially for light, limber spinning rods.

On baitcasting and spincast rod handles, the locking screw and reel-clamping devices vary widely these days in both design and quality. The main requirement is that the device hold the reel steadily and securely, and I would advise anyone to test his reel on a new rod before buying it. My personal preference is for a simple screw that goes directly through the rod handle from the underside and threads directly into a reel-clamp block. I favor this uncomplicated design because it is, in my opinion, generally trouble-free.

Frankly, I mistrust any reel-locking mechanism that depends on longitudinal thrust. Although there are some good rods with this type of locking mechanism, I have good reason to be suspicious of them. As I pointed out in my book *Fishing for Bass,* I had a great deal of trouble with such a mechanism on a rod that was made by an old and (I thought) reliable firm. The reel kept jumping out of the seat. It jumped out on my wife while she was doing battle with an 8-pound largemouth, and I vowed to get rid of the thing. But I liked the action and weight of the rod and hated to throw it away. So, I discarded the parts of the reel-clamp mechanism, drilled a hole through the reel-seat saddle, and drilled another hole through the foot of an old Ambassadeur reel. Then I attached the reel to the rod with a nut and bolt! Of course, I don't advise another angler to drill his rod and reel. But I do think that this nut-and-bolt locking system is a good design, and I, for one, have a rod and reel outfit that doesn't jiggle, wiggle, or fall apart!

2

Rod Blanks

To the tournament casting buff, the sole purpose of a rod is to help cast a weight. To the fisherman, however, the rod is not only a casting aid but also a means of imparting action and direction to a lure, a lever for setting the hook, and a shock absorber for fighting and landing fish. The requirements of a good bass fishing rod and a good casting rod are not always the same, and may not even be compatible, as in the case of extremely stiff worm rods. I personally feel that most bass rods are too stiff, but this is something that each angler should decide for himself. Here are some points to consider:

Action. Modern rods are usually classified as slow, medium, fast, and extra-fast, depending on how they bend when you are casting lures or baits. A slow rod bends from tip to butt, and an extra-fast rod bends only in the tip quarter. The four actions are shown graphically in the accompanying illustration, but remember that the rod in motion during a cast is a dynamic thing, not a static one.

Although the four classifications of action do reflect a rod's taper, it is best to consider action in terms of time. To be of maximum use during a cast, a rod must bend. If it doesn't bend, it is nothing more than a

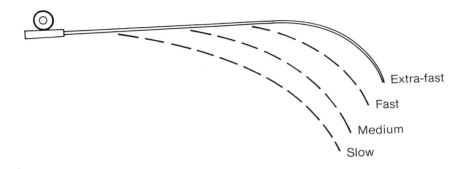

lever used to sling a lure out by sheer muscle power. Although an angler could get a lure out a respectable distance with a 6-foot rigid lever, he would have little control over where it went, and he would have to sling it out with his arm instead of casting it with "a flip of the wrist." When the rod bends, however, it stores the angler's muscular energy. The rod then recoils and uses this stored energy to propel the lure forward. This is where the element of time comes in. The time span required for bending and recoil in a slow rod is longer than in a fast rod.

The advantage in having a slow rod is that the angler has more control of the lure and can cast with less effort. The disadvantage of the fast rod is that the angler must make quick, snappy casts and has to wield the rod more forcefully. Using more muscle in a shorter time span adversely affects both casting ease and accuracy.

From the standpoint of casting, an extra-fast rod is an absurdity. A 6-foot rod with all the action in the last 1½ feet is nothing more than a 1½-foot casting rod with a 4½-foot lever on it. Yet, the extra-fast rod has been quite popular with bass anglers for the past few years, and some of the better tackle companies still manufacture them in large numbers. So many anglers have gone for the "quick taper" design that it is sometimes difficult to find a slower rod in a tackle shop! The sales pitch is that these rods have a fast tip for casting and a heavy mid- and butt section for setting the hook and horsing bass out of thick cover. The plain truth is that anglers—especially bass anglers—are too quick to buy newfangled gear. We are a faddish bunch.

Author's nephew, David Livingston, uses a rather stiff rod to horse a bass out of a partly submerged treetop. He is fishing from his Stump Knocker boat on Alabama's little Choctawhatchee River.

Weight. Regardless of action, different rod blanks are designed to handle lures of different weights. In other words, one may have two rods of equal length and the same action that have vastly different casting properties. Even though the action on both may be slow, one rod might be stiff and the other limber. This is strictly a matter of stiffness and has nothing to do with "action" or which portion of the rod bends. Generally speaking, weight designates the weight of the lure required to bend the rod sufficiently for the cast. A light rod, then, would be limber so that a light lure would bend it during the cast; a heavy rod would be rather stiff so that only a heavy lure would bend it during the cast. One simply can't cast properly by using a heavy lure on a light rod, or a light lure on a heavy rod.

In fact, the weight of the lure to be cast should be the determining factor in the choice of a casting rod. But few anglers ever consult the manufacturers' catalogs or data sheets before buying a rod off a rack in a tackle shop. The specification of the weight or power of a rod is not uniform throughout the industry, so that the following tables are only approximate. (Note also that the figures below will not be valid unless the reel is *fully* spooled with the proper *weight* line.)

Baitcasting and Spincast

Rod Weight	Lure Weight (ounces)
Ultralight	⅛ to ¼
Light	¼ to ½
Medium	⅝ to ¾
Heavy	¾ to 1¼
Worm	?

Freshwater Spinning

Rod Weight	Lure Weight (ounces)
Ultralight	1/16 to ⅛
Extralight	1/16 to ¼
Light	⅛ to ⅜
Medium light	¼ to ½
Medium	⅜ to ⅝
Heavy	½ to 1
Worm	?

I have left a question mark beside the worm rods in the tables; classification is difficult because some brands of worm rod are stiffer than others. Although a few worm rods will cast heavy lures satisfactorily, most of them are so stiff that it would take a half-pound lure and some muscle to bend them properly for the cast! Strictly from a casting viewpoint, the worm rod is ridiculous. From a fishing viewpoint, however, the worm rod has a big advantage over limber sticks in that it is ideal for setting a hook. This hook-setting ability is very important in worm fishing for two reasons. First, the worm is rigged on a large hook, and it is always harder to set a large hook than a small one. Second, the hook must be set in spite of a wire weed guard, or, when using the Texas rig, it must be jerked through the worm body (or part of it) before it sticks the bass. The alternative to a stiff rod is to let the bass "run" until it swallows the worm. The disadvantage of this is that the bass may spit out the worm (especially if it is weighted) or it will be gut-hooked. More and more anglers are releasing all or part of their catch these days, and gut-hooked bass are less likely to live. Also, a gut-hooked lunker bass is more likely to abrade the angler's line and break off. It seems, then, that a stiff rod is a necessary evil in worm fishing. But I think that most of them are a lot stiffer than necessary.

One claim that is frequently made in favor of the worm rod is that it is highly desirable to help horse a lunker bass out of thick cover or up from underwater brush. Personally, I don't subscribe to this because I believe that a medium-weight baitcasting rod is just as effective in working bass out of thick stuff. A modern rod will take a lot of pressure, and a good fiberglass blank free of defects will put one's line to test.

I own a worm rod, and I use it from time to time. But in all honesty I wouldn't advise a newcomer to the sport to purchase one, simply because it is impossible to learn to cast properly with a worm rod. I would advise him to buy a medium-weight rod. If he ties a worm onto the end of his line, however, I would advise him strongly to hone the hook down to needle-point sharpness.

Finally, let me suggest that a medium rod with a reel spooled with low-stretch dacron line will hook just as many bass as worm rods used with stretchy monofilament. As will be discussed in Chapter 5, I often use dacron line with a baitcasting rig, but I do usually tie a short monofilament leader to the end of it.

Length. As a general rule, a long rod will cast further than a short one simply because the angler has more leverage. Another general rule is that the lighter the lure, the longer the rod should be. But of course there are practical limits to rod length, and the angler's comfort must be considered in rod design. Most of the ultralight baitcasting rods are from 6 to 6½ feet long; light, from 5½ to 6½; medium, from 4 to 6½; heavy, from 4½ to 7½. (Heavy baitcasting rods over 6 feet long are designed with long handles to facilitate two-handed casting.) Spinning rods used for most bass fishing run from about 5½ to 7 feet long.

In almost all cases, a rod about 6 feet long casts better than one much longer or much shorter. Most bass anglers don't use rods longer than 6 feet, but some do often use short "brush rods" for fishing small streams and the shoreline of some lakes. A short rod, if properly used, casts a lure in a lower trajectory, thereby permitting the angler to get back under overhanging brush better than he could with a long rod. My only advice on this point is to get a brush rod with slow action, one that flexes from tip to butt, so that you can cast a lure accurately with it.

For general fishing, a long rod is better than a short one of similar action and weight simply because it is capable of hooking more fish. The tip of a long rod makes a wider arc when the angler sets the hook, and the wider arc hauls in more slack line quicker and helps get the stretch out of monofilament.

Ferrules. In rods that break down into two or more pieces for ease of storage and transportation, male and female ferrules must be used to join one piece to the other. Ferrules present some headaches for the rod maker, and some pains in the neck for the angler. Often they bind and stick together. Sometimes either the female or the male ferrule becomes loose on the blank—which can cause the rod to snap in two. (It is a good idea to carry a stick of ferrule cement in your tackle box if your rods have metal ferrules; a loose ferrule should be fixed immediately.) They will sometimes wear so much that they cause a "slap" in the rod during the cast. And any ferrule, especially a cheap metal one, will create a blank spot in the rod; the ferrule joint doesn't bend with the rest of the rod, or doesn't bend as much.

Personally, I solved all my ferrule problems by refusing to buy anything but one-piece rod blanks (except in fly rods). A one-piece rod is stronger and lighter and cheaper to manufacture. The storage and transportation of one-piece rods is not often a problem for me, and many anglers who own big bass boats with lockable rod compartments simply leave their rods in the boat at all times. Whatever the reason, there is definitely a trend toward one-piece spinning and casting rods these days, and some top-quality casting rods even have fixed handles.

But one-piece rods are not practical for everyone. Many anglers want, and need, a break-apart rod for storage in the trunk of their car, and some want many-pieced backpack or briefcase rods. For what it's worth, my personal choice is a glass-to-glass ferrule—but maybe I have been rather gullible in this matter. Because I seldom use ferrules these days, and could well be wrong about glass-to-glass, I would like to quote at length from Dale P. Clemens' *Fiberglass Rod Making*:

The most recent development in fiberglass rods has been the so-called "non-ferrule" connection or glass-to-glass ferrule. This design was first introduced by some of the best manufacturers and has gained so much popularity that most companies have begun to utilize it in their top-of-the-line rods. While it has some advantages, it has disadvantages too, and I feel that the value of the glass-to-glass ferrule has been exaggerated. . . .

To understand this aspect of rod construction more fully, we need to examine the history and function of the ferrule. The ideal rod would be of one piece its entire length, so as to fully preserve the smooth bending and action. However, because of the practical considerations of storage and transportation, this is generally ruled out. We need a rod that will break down into two or more sections, which necessitates some kind of slip joint. For years this joint was accomplished with a metal ferrule. On quality bamboo rods, it was always made of nickel silver. This is an alloy consisting of 18 percent nickel, 12–18 percent zinc, and the balance copper. It does not fatigue easily, has high tensile strength, and is reasonably light in weight.

A lesser-quality ferrule was frequently used on many earlier glass production rods. It was nickel-plated brass, cheaper and heavier, and definitely had both limited strength and life.

In recent years an exciting new metal ferrule has appeared. Anodized aluminum alloys are now used by Featherweight Products to make a ferrule that is 300 percent lighter and 25 percent stronger than nickel-plated brass. These are machined with a silken-smooth cushion fit made possible by a slight taper on the male and female pieces, and utilize a replaceable rubber 0-ring on the slide (male piece). They are lighter than, and compare quite favorably with, the more expensive nickel-silver ferrules. If the rod is to be used in salt water, they are preferable by far, since nickel silver is extremely vulnerable to corrosion in salt water.

Shorter metal ferrules of all three metals have been introduced. These are often called "mini-ferrules" or "micro-ferrules." Their shorter length reduces the flat spot somewhat, but only at the price of reduced strength. As a result their use is confined to very light rods for delicate fishing.

In an attempt to utilize the flexibility and strength of fiberglass itself, a ferrule was developed which used a metal plug permanently affixed within the tube of one rod section. The open tube of the blank of the other rod section slipped over this metal plug, which was built with a taper to perfectly match the tube into which it fit. This is the metal-to-glass ferrule still in much use. However, as in all ferrule joints using the fiberglass tube of the blank, the walls had to be reinforced in some way or they would split under heavy bending pressure. This reinforcement is accomplished with either extra glass around the walls of the joint or a double layer of thread wrapping.

Instead of a metal plug, if one of solid fiberglass is used, an entirely glass-to-glass joint results. All other aspects of this ferrule are the same as the metal-to-glass ferrule.

Two additional glass ferrules were developed. One utilizes a fiberglass sleeve which has one half glued over the tip section of the blank, forming a glass socket or female ferrule. The forward end of the butt section of the blank becomes the male ferrule, which slides into the sleeve. The other type of glass-to-glass joint must be manufactured on two separate mandrels, one for each section of the blank. This obviously increases the cost of this type of rod. The design consists of a tip section whose lower end terminates in a large enough diameter to allow it to slip over the forward end of the butt section. In effect, the lower end becomes a female ferrule.

If we are going to get this ferrule question in proper perspective, we must realize that regardless of the material used—metal, metal to glass, or glass to glass—there is always a more rigid section involved. In the case of glass, it may be a solid glass plug or the double walls where hollow glass fits over hollow glass. *Any* ferrule results in more rigidity at the joint.

The proponents of glass-to-glass connections will claim that solid fiberglass plugs and reinforced fiberglass walls will flex better than metal. Even over the few short inches occupied by the ferrule, I suppose that if some sort of delicate scientific test were run, this could be proved—but I do not think it really matters a bit when it gets down to the practicability of actual casting. There are other advantages and disadvantages of glass-to-glass ferrules, but in all honesty I do not think casting is really one of them. In fact, a well-known consumer testing service just recently tested 35 different makes of fiberglass fly rods which included all of the previously described type of ferrules. When it came down to any relationship that might exist between ferrule design and performance in casting, they could draw no conclusions based on their tests. All cast equally well.

The primary merits of a glass connection are that it makes a neat, hardly noticeable joint, and is lighter than plated brass or nickel silver. The latter advantage of weight saving at the ferrule can alter the balance of the rod and give it a different "feel" in the hand of the caster. However, there is little noticeable weight saving over the new (anodized-aluminum-alloy) ferrules. The tapered fiberglass-to-fiberglass ferrules and the aluminum ferrules with 0-ring are both easier to use and more resistant to dirt fouling than the other ferrules.

There are some disadvantages of glass ferrules that the advertising people do not talk about. For one thing, the joint tends to loosen sooner than metal and no longer provides a tight fit. Unfortunately, when that happens there is little that can be done about it. Metal ferrule joints can also loosen in time, but the ferrule itself is easily replaced. An aluminum-alloy ferrule with rubber 0-ring can often be restored to a tight fit merely by replacing the 0-ring. With a glass connection you face a serious problem if one section of the glass ferrule splits, or becomes cracked or broken. Since the female or tube end is the most vulnerable, it is generally placed on the tip section. So, a broken glass ferrule means replacing the entire tip section of the rod—assuming a replacment is still available.

About 95 percent of all modern fishing rods are made from fiberglass, although the new graphite rods may change this. Steel and tubular steel rods are things of the past. Bamboo is still used in some of the more expensive fly rods because some serious fly-fishermen prefer it over fiberglass and are willing to pay for it, but bamboo spinning or casting rods are seldom seen these days.

The virtues of fiberglass are many. It is strong, light, tough, waterproof, and impervious to salt and most other commonly encountered elements. It is resilient and does not "set" or warp from long use or improper storage. Moreover, fiberglass rod blanks can be more or less mass-produced.

Construction techniques vary considerably, but in the simplest terms a fiberglass blank is made by winding glass-fiber cloth around a tapered mandrel, impregnating the fibers with a resin, and then setting the blank under heat and pressure. The properties of the finished blank depend on the wall thickness, on the length and taper of the mandrel, on the types of fiberglass and resins used, on the proportion of fiberglass to resin, and on refinements in construction technique.

Owing largely to improved materials and refined methods of manufacture, fiberglass rods have become steadily better and better during the past 25 years. And improvements continue. Orvis, for example, says that their Golden Eagle rods are made of recently developed high-density glass and are set under a pressure of 2,000 pounds per square inch in a process that removes all microscopic air bubbles, which can cause dead spots or weak areas in the blank. St. Croix has a new process that puts three times as many glass fibers in a blank, resulting in greater strength at less weight. Other firms have similar claims, and all make the best possible rod.

Many of the older rods had hard spots in the blank because of manufacturing imperfections of one sort or another. Once, when fishing in the Florida Keys, I broke a brand-new rod simply by casting out a live shrimp. Inspection showed that there was a hard, brittle spot in the blank. This sort of thing may still occur, but it's not as frequent as it once was.

One problem with today's rods, however, is that some of them have a large diameter and thin walls on the butt end. I broke one of these not long ago, but it was a cheap rod to begin with. And just the other day I saw a guy charging into a discount store with a broken rod in his hand. I understand that this problem is so common with some of the cheaper rods that some tackle shops are refusing to stock them. I don't think there is too much of a problem with the better rods, most of which are covered by a guarantee. But it is a point worth keeping in mind: Any lightweight rod that has a large butt diameter has got to have thin walls.

Although most of the fiberglass rods used for bass fishing are tubular and have a hollow core from butt to tip, there are a few solid glass rods around. Solid glass rods of good quality are stronger than tubular rods, but they are also much heavier. Most of the top-quality solid glass rods being built today are intended for saltwater use, and most of the lighter freshwater solid glass rods found in discount stores are $2.98 junk.

Although tubular fiberglass is probably the most practical material for both spinning and casting rods, it may not be the ultimate. Developed in aerospace research, a new material called high-modulus graphite has recently been introduced in the Fenwick line. They now have production models available at from $150 to $200, and they aren't likely to get much cheaper because of manufacturing difficulties. Although I feel that high-modulus graphite is too expensive for practical fishing, it is nevertheless magic stuff, and I don't see how the complete bass angler can continue to function without owning two or three.

The graphite rods are made of polyacrylonitrile filaments, which look like fine silken threads. According to Union Carbide Corporation, the strands have a tensile strength of 360,000 psi and an elastic modulus of 32 million psi! The best comparison to fiberglass that I've seen was in an article by Nick Sisley in the *American Bass Fisherman* (November/December 1974). He arbitrarily gave fiberglass a "specific strength" and a "specific flexural modulus" (resistance to bending) of 1.0; by comparison, high-modulus graphite would have a specific strength of 2.9 and a specific flexural modulus of 4.1. In other words, the stuff is very strong and very stiff for its weight.

Typically, a rod blank is about 33 percent smaller in diameter and about 25 percent lighter than a comparable fiberglass blank. The weight of the blank, however, isn't the whole story. When the weights of the guides, tip, handle, and wrappings are figured in, a graphite rod is not 25 percent lighter than a comparable fiberglass rod. But the finished graphite rods *are* lighter, and this is important to some anglers —especially those who compete in tournaments.

When an angler first picks up a graphite rod, he notes its small diameter and lightness; then he is somewhat surprised by its stiffness. This impression of stiffness can be misleading because it is difficult to tell how a graphite rod will cast merely by picking one up in a tackle shop and swishing it about. The material is so different from fiberglass that its true casting properties aren't apparent until the rod is loaded with line and lure. For this reason, I would recommend that the prospective angler test a graphite rod with a practice plug before buying it.

The graphite rods also have a fast recovery rate, and the problem of vibration is not as severe as it is in fiberglass rods. Quickly dampening the vibration reduces line slap and helps eliminate waves in a line during the cast. The faster recovery rate also tends to produce more distance and a lower trajectory.

Most of the articles and promotional material that I've seen on high-modulus graphite say that the faster recovery rate makes for improved accuracy in casting, but I'm not yet sold on this. I can see how dampening the vibration would indeed improve accuracy, but being faster in terms of release would, it seems to me, make the timing more critical than with a slower material such as fiberglass. And yet I think there's something here that hasn't been explained, and it could well be that high-modulus graphite makes a whole new ball game for rod designers and theorists. From a sort of field-test viewpoint, my impression is that the graphite rods are indeed more accurate than fiberglass. I have cast extensively with a *light* Fenwick HMG baitcasting rod, and I will say that it is the most accurate rod I've ever used. But this is just one rod, and one angler. To say categorically that graphite is more accurate than fiberglass would be going too far at this time. I will say that most of the graphite blanks currently on the market are far too stiff to suit me.

In any case, casting isn't the only consideration. A big advantage of graphite is that it is more sensitive to vibrations transmitted up the line. Thus, the angler has a better feeling for what his lure is doing, which can be quite important when one is "feeling out" submerged structure. A graphite rod and dacron line make a spinnerbait or sonic lure with a tight wiggle seem alive during the retrieve, so that the angler somehow fishes with more confidence. This sensitivity can also be very important in detecting light "strikes" in cold water or when fishing plastic worms or fall baits.

Still another advantage is that graphite rods permit the angler to set the hook a little faster. Few anglers realize it, but when they set the hook hard with a fiberglass rod, the tip actually dips in the opposite direction. (To test this, hold a limber fiberglass rod an inch off the floor and parallel to the floor. Jerk up on the handle and note that the tip will strike the floor before it starts upwards.) Graphite rods, on the other hand, have less of this countermovement or back-snap, which makes the angler a little faster on the strike. Anyone who has ever seen a bass engulf a lure and spit it out before he could set the hook knows that a split second can be important!

Although I do have some puzzling reservations about graphite's speed of recovery and its relation to casting accuracy, my conclusion is that these new rods have some highly desirable qualities. I hope that the price will come down, and that a wider range of blanks will be made available. At the time of this writing, Fenwick has several casting and spinning rods on the market. Fenwick, Orvis, Leonard's, Shakespeare, and possibly other firms have high-modulus graphite fly rods in production, and Gene Bullard Custom Rods reported that they are making more and more custom jobs on graphite blanks. The trend is likely to continue, slowly and cautiously. I read recently that Fenwick has predicted that by 1980 about half of all rod blanks will be made from high-modulus graphite. Maybe. But the stuff will have to get cheaper.

3

Baitcasting
Reels

ALMOST ALL BASS PROS, commercial guides, and knowledgeable amateurs rely on good baitcasting rigs. They may have ultralight or heavy-duty spinning outfits for special purposes or unusual conditions, but most of their fishing is done with modern free-spooling baitcasting reels that cost $50 or more. The main advantage of baitcasting reels over spinning or spincast reels is that they are more accurate. The reason that they are more accurate is that the angler can "thumb" the revolving spool, and this sense of touch permits greater control over the lure.

The accuracy of the baitcasting reel makes it ideally suited for plugging the shoreline or any type of visible cover. I have fished in some spots where accuracy was of utmost importance. On some clear-water streams, for example, a cast that does not place the lure within 6 inches of target is wasted. This sort of pinpoint accuracy is not so important for some applications, such as jump fishing for schooling bass or even for working invisible underwater structure. (To be sure, accuracy is important when fishing underwater structure, simply because the lure has got to get in close to the bass, but a different sort of skill and sense is required for this.) In some cases, spinning gear works as well as, or better than, baitcasting outfits. Still, if all the expert bassmen in the country had to choose one rig, an overwhelming number of them would pick a baitcasting reel and a fairly stiff rod. They like

This happy angler used a baitcasting reel to catch this lunker largemouth. Most bassmen prefer baitcasting gear.

the accuracy, the sense of control, the feeling of always being in touch with their lure.

Another big but untouted advantage of a baitcasting reel is that it causes less wear and tear on one's fishing line. One reason for this is that the line comes off a revolving spool in a straight and sensible manner, whereas line comes off a fixed-spool reel in coils and must be funneled through the guides toward the tip of the rod. Another reason is that baitcasting reels wind the line directly onto the revolving spool, whereas line being retrieved on a spinning or spincast reel must be turned 90 degrees and pulled over some sort of line-wearing guide or post. Although some of the better spinning reels have roller line guides, the fact remains that line must be pulled over metal at a severe angle.

The big disadvantage of baitcasting reels is that they are difficult to use properly, as compared to spinning and spincast gear. This is a disadvantage that the bass angler will do well to overcome. And it's not as hard as many people believe it to be, especially with the modern freespooling reels with built-in antibacklash devices. The basic steps of baitcasting are set forth in the manuals provided with the better reels, and the novice should practice them. Any angler who has trouble with accuracy should take a new look at the basics and ask himself whether he is *casting* a lure or merely slinging it out. If improperly used, even the finest baitcasting reel isn't any more accurate than a push-button spincast outfit.

Also, there is no point in having an expensive, precision reel unless the angler keeps it in excellent working condition. A fine reel should be oiled after (or before) each fishing trip, and always after long storage, according to the manufacturer's instructions. But don't clog the reel with oil or grease, and be sure to clean it frequently. Parts susceptible to wear or damage, such as the paul and the drag washers, should be replaced often.

Further, there is little point in having such features as adjustable drags and brakes unless the angler understands them, the way they work, and when they should be adjusted to accommodate different weights of line and lure.

It would take a whole book and a thousand illustrations to describe and discuss fully all the moving parts in a modern baitcasting reel. I have therefore limited the discussions that follow to the parts, mechanisms, and related topics that will in my opinion help the angler to know his reel better and to use it to fuller advantage.

Top: A typical free-spooling baitcasting reel with a star drag.
Bottom: New direct-drive free-spooling reel.

Clutch and antireverse device. All modern free-spooling reels have a clutch to disengage the drive gears and handle during the cast. This design is a tremendous advantage over the less sophisticated casting reels, on which the reel handle as well as the drive gears turn during the cast. The free-spooling reels permit more distance, are less inclined to backlash, and work better in every way. Although they're a good deal more expensive, they're worth it.

To disengage the gears and handle on most free-spooling reels, the angler merely presses a conveniently located button or lever. After the cast, the gears and handle are automatically engaged when the angler turns the reel handle forward to start the retrieve.

The same clutch mechanism also acts as an antireverse device, which permits the handle of the reel to turn in only one direction. In other words, a big bass can't jerk the handle out of your hand. On older reels, the handle can be turned either way, and it wasn't uncommon for an angler to lose hold on the handle when a lunker bass hit. Anyone who has ever busted his knuckles trying to stop a whirling handle knows the value of an antireverse device!

Level-wind mechanism. Almost all bass anglers are quite familiar with the mechanism that winds the line smoothly and evenly onto the spool. Newcomers to the art of baitcasting will quickly become familiar with the level wind simply because it is the most frequent cause of unsmooth casting and of backlash. Apart from the line carriage and the housing, the main components of the level-wind mechanism are a paul and a double-threaded shaft, often called the worm.

The paul is of primary concern because it is the part of the reel that is most likely to wear quickly. Both the paul and the worm should be lubricated (lightly) during each fishing trip, and at least twice during all-day trips. Even if the paul is kept lubricated, it should be replaced after a few months of hard fishing. Pauls are cheap, so buy half a dozen and keep them in your tackle box.

The worm may need replacing from time to time, but not nearly as often as the paul. The important thing to remember about the worm is that it *must* be kept clean and well lubricated. Because the level-wind mechanism is open on the bottom, the worm is likely to accumulate dust, which, together with the lubricating oil, can form a goo that slows down the paul and impedes the cast. Always clean the worm after a reel has been dropped in sand or dirt. I clean mine with lighter fluid and an old toothbrush. Gasoline will do a good job. After cleaning the worm, I spray it with WD-40. During a fishing trip, I lubricate the worm with one drop of reel oil. Some anglers use a light grease, but I prefer the oil, especially in cold weather.

In most level-wind mechanisms, the line guide moves back and forth on the cast as well as on the retrieve. One exception is the Shakespeare "total free spool" design, in which the line guide and the paul remain stationary during the cast. (Heddon has recently come out with a similar reel.) One big advantage of this design is that a worn paul or dirty worm will have no adverse effect on the cast itself. Another advantage, of course, is that the paul and worm will not wear as quickly.

Still another advantage is that no energy is used up to operate the level-wind mechanism during the cast, but this saving in energy is offset (to some degree) by the drag and friction of the line going through the stationary line guide. I don't have any engineering data on how much energy is wasted by one mechanism or the other, but I have tested a Shakespeare that belongs to a friend of mine; it casts smoothly enough, and isn't short on distance. If I owned one, however, I would keep a close eye on the circular line guide. It, like the rings in rod guides and tips, is bound to wear somewhat from all that line shooting out on first one side and then the other; and a worn or grooved line guide is bound to abrade a fishing line.

Mechanical brake. The better reels have a knob to adjust "end play" tension on the spool axles. If the knob is too loose, there will be some noticeable end play in the spool; if it is too tight, the spool will not turn freely enough for casting. If it is too loose, the spool is likely to overspin and cause backlash; if too tight, casting distance and accuracy are limited. Ideally, the tension should be adjusted for each lure. The adjustment knobs are usually calibrated, and one can remember the settings for each lure or can make measurable adjustments during test casts.

A good rule of thumb is to adjust the tension device so that a particular lure will barely turn the spool when the reel's gears are disengaged. The procedure is simply to hold the rod straight out, reel the lure to within a few inches of the rod tip, depress the free-spooling button, and let the lure drop by its own weight. If it does not drop at all, loosen the knob until the lure's weight starts it down. If it drops too fast, tighten the knob a bit. Another rule of thumb is that the lure should not fall so fast that it causes overspin when it hits the floor or ground. The optimum rate of fall will vary somewhat from one angler to another. I personally vary the fall rate with different types of lure of the same weight. A ½-ounce jig, for example, has little air resistance during the cast and should have a relatively tight setting, whereas a ½-ounce balsa plug has a lot of air resistance and should have a relatively loose setting. Rod action and length, line weight and limpness, and the individual's casting skill also have a bearing on ideal tension settings for each lure.

The mechanical brake is not a complicated mechanism and requires little maintenance. For repeatable performance at the various calibrated settings, however, the mechanism should be oiled frequently, or according to the manufacturer's instructions.

Centrifugal brake. The better baitcasting reels have both a mechanical brake and a centrifugal brake or spool drag. The centrifugal mechanism is primarily an antibacklash device that prevents the spool from overspinnning. The faster the spool turns, the greater the braking force; the slower the spool turns, the less the braking force.

The centrifugal brake is a highly desirable feature for newcomers to the art of baitcasting because it can virtually eliminate backlash. With

Typical brake blocks on an antibacklash device in free-spooling reels.

properly adjusted reels and matching tackle, it is indeed possible to make a long cast without even touching the spool with the thumb! Try that with older reels with whirling handles and you'll likely spend the rest of the day trying to untangle your line.

As shown in the accompanying photograph, the centrifugal brake mechanism consists of cylindrical brake blocks free-floating on a long pin attached to the spool shaft. As the spool turns, the blocks slide outward (because of centrifugal force) until they come into contact with a stationary drum flange. The ends of the blocks turning against the drum create friction, and the frictional drag is proportional to the speed of the reel spool.

The photograph shows the centrifugal brake system used in the Ambassadeur 5000 and 6000 reels. The two brake blocks on the pin can be removed, and this permits blocks of various sizes to be used. Garcia markets replacement blocks in three weights in order to allow for adjustment. It is also possible to vary the number as well as the size of the blocks. How many and what size blocks a particular angler should use depends not only on his lure, rod action, and line size but also on his skill at casting. The greater his skill, the smaller and fewer the cylinders that are needed. It's a neat system, but I doubt that very many anglers take the trouble to change blocks with different lures or different rod actions. I don't, at least not often. It's too easy to make adjustments on the mechanical brake! For a long while I used only two small cylinders for all my lures. Then I lost one of the blocks when taking the reel apart (I seem to lose at least one each time I go into an Ambassadeur) and couldn't find a replacement in my repair kit. For a long while I used the reel with only one block, and it worked fine. When writing this chapter, I took the reel apart to study the mechanism—and lost the other brake. I've ordered some replacements, but in the meantime I've been using the reel without any blocks at all. It works very well, but the spool does tend to overspin. So far I've avoided a serious backlash; in fact, I have never had a serious backlash with a modern free-spooling baitcasting reel.

Retrieve ratio. The rate at which a lure is retrieved through the water depends on how fast the reel handle is cranked, on the diameter of the spool and how full of line it is, and on the retrieve ratio of the reel. The retrieve ratio is determined by the gearing in the drive mechanism, and it can vary considerably. The Pflueger Akron has a ratio of 4 to 1; the Ambassadeur 5000, 3.6 to 1; and so on. Many of the new reels have ratios of almost 5 to 1.

The thinking behind the high-speed reels is that the angler can work fast-moving baits without having to crank so frantically. These reels are ideal for working surface-buzzing lures, skitter spoons, and other baits that must be retrieved fast, but they may not be the best choice for an angler who has only one general-purpose reel. In my opinion, they are far from ideal for working crankbaits, spinnerbaits with large blades, and other lures that are hard to pull in. The higher the retrieve ratio, the harder it is to turn the handle. Although this wouldn't be too important for a few casts, it can become a fatigue factor during a long day's fishing. Yet, many anglers are buying these new high-speed reels specifically for fishing crankbaits and spinnerbaits because they can get more speed with them. What many of these anglers fail to consider is that they can't have both speed and power from one set of gears. So, if you are in the market for a new free-spooler for fishing fast baits, make up your mind whether you want to crank faster or harder.

High-speed replacement gears. Most of the baitcasting reels on the market a few years ago had a standard retrieve ratio of about 3.5 to 1. When the newer high-speed jobs came out, I wanted one immediately because I often fish with a very fast retrieve. When I checked the price of the new reels, however, I decided to try the high-speed replacement

High-speed replacement gears for a free-spooling baitcasting reel.

gears marketed by Lew Childre and Cordell Tackle (and possibly by other firms). They work satisfactorily, saved me about $50, and gave a new life to my old Ambassadeur 5000A.

High-speed replacement gears are available for the Daiwa Millionaire reels and for the following Ambassadeur models: 5000, 5000A, 5000B, 5000C, 5000D, 5001, 6000, and 6000C. One big advantage of these gears is that if you don't like the fast retrieve you can always put the old ones back in.

Bearings. Many of the top-quality baitcasting reels have ball bearings fitted around the spool axles, whereas other reels operate on a shaft and bushing principle. There is no doubt that ball bearings work a little smoother on the cast and on the retrieve. But I could get along without them, and for a number of years I did just that. Some anglers and reel manufacturers may jump up and down at what I am about to say, but I sometimes wonder whether ball bearings are worth the extra money. Maybe I'm missing something, but I don't see too much advantage in speeding a spool up with ball bearings and then slowing it down with a mechanical brake. This is rather like mashing the accelerator of an automobile and applying the brake at the same time. But ball bearings probably work a little better, and may last longer, since the friction is distributed over a larger surface area.

And there may be more subtle design reasons for having ball bearings. Because pressure is exerted on the bearings and shaft from different points on the spool (depending on where the line is at any one moment), there must be some degree of "play." I haven't looked closely into this problem, but the 5000 has "floating bushings to support the spool axle," and the Daiwa Millionaire V has "balanced spherical ball bearings, the system that's self-aligning no matter what pressure is exerted on a particular portion of the spool."

Spooling. It is important that the spool of a baitcasting reel be kept full of line. A full spool not only makes casting easier and increases distance but also saves wear and tear on the paul and other moving parts. Look at some figures. If a full spool is 2 inches in diameter, it will lay out 6.28 inches of line per revolution at the beginning of the cast. But if it is filled only to ¼ inch from the top, it will lay out only 4.71 inches per revolution at the beginning of the cast. Thus, a full spool will cast a given distance with fewer and *slower* revolutions. (A full spool also, in effect, gives the line more "leverage" with which to overcome the inertia of the spool; on the other hand, the inertia of the spool is increased by the weight of the line wound around it.)

Another advantage of a full spool is that it increases the rate of retrieve, which can be important with fast-moving lures such as the Weed Wing. (Anglers who own the new high-speed reels should note that having a depleted spool will quickly offset the advantages of a high gear ratio.) In addition to permitting the angler to move the lure faster, increasing the rate of retrieve will reduce the number of revolutions required to retrieve a lure a given distance, which, in turn, reduces wear and tear on gears, pauls, and other moving parts.

The only disadvantage of a full spool is that the line is more likely to bind between the spool and the reel housing. Most of the better reels are designed to minimize this problem, and it has happened to me only a few times. It can, however, cause severe backlash and can damage one's line.

Reel arbors. A reel spool acts somewhat like a flywheel. The heavier it is, the harder it is to start and stop. A lighter spool not only permits easier casting and more distance but also reduces the risk of backlash. Thanks to free-spooling reels with antibacklash devices, the problem of spool weight is not as important as it once was, but it is still a consideration, especially if the angler wants to cast light lures on a baitcasting rig.

One way to reduce the total weight of the reel spool is to limit the amount of line on it, but a half-full spool is not desirable, for reasons already discussed. The way to reduce the amount of line and still have a full spool is to install an arbor made of cork (or balsa). In addition to making the spool lighter, the arbor will save the angler a good deal of money on fishing line. The Ambassadeur 5000, for example, holds about 200 yards of 10-pound line, whereas 50 yards is plenty for practical bass fishing.

Pflueger still offers cork arbors for some of their reels, but most manufacturers no longer provide accessory arbors. It may be possible to find an arbor in a good tackle shop or in a mail-order catalog. Arbors can be made from cork rings intended to be used on rod handles, but they require a good deal of custom fitting.

Power handles. A friend of mine paid over $60 for a new reel, and the first time he tied into a lunker bass the handle bent on him. He was angry, to say the least. I told him that he could purchase a new, oversized power handle for the reel. He was glad to get this information, but he felt that the company that made the $60 reel should have put a good handle on it in the first place. I agree. The small handles found on some reels are probably carryovers from the days when the drive gears and handle turned during the cast.

In any case, power handles are quite popular among bass anglers. They are easier to use, especially for night fishing, and somehow give the angler more command over his tackle. And over lunker bass. For one thing, the longer handle has more leverage. For another, the large, oversized handle knob is less likely to slip out of the angler's grip. Most of these handles cost only a couple of bucks, and they are surely worth it, especially for reels having 5-to-1 retrieve ratios. Lindy's, Cordell

Most bassmen prefer large power handles and replace the small handles that come on some baitcasting reels.

Tackle, Zorro, and a number of other firms offer power handles, and they are widely available in tackle shops and through mail-order houses. Also, some reel makers offer power handles as either standard or optional for some of their reels.

Drag. Most expensive baitcasting reels of today have a good star drag system. The term "star drag" is used because of the starlike shape of the external adjusting wheel, located just under the reel handle. This shape is desirable because it enables the angler to make adjustments on the drag with thumb or finger while doing battle with a large fish.

Many anglers do not realize it, but on star drag reels the handle turns the spool solely by a frictional drive mechanism. The friction is created by washers under pressure or compression. The tighter the star drag is set, the greater this compression. If the drag is set too tight, the line will break before the washers slip; if the drag is set too loose, there won't be enough frictional contact to turn the weight of the spool, much less check the run of a large fish. The exact setting of the drag should depend on the weight of the angler's line and where he is fishing. I use a rather light drag setting in open water, but I tighten down considerably when fishing in treetops or heavy cover.

Most anglers test their drag setting merely by stripping line off the reel, failing to realize that the reel drag is only a part of the total drag exerted on a line. A good deal of drag is created when the line goes over the rod guides and tip; the higher the rod is held while fighting a fish, the greater this drag becomes. Drag is also caused by line being pulled through the water. (Anyone who doubts this should let out 50 yards of line and run the boat at high speed.) In any case, most anglers knowingly or unknowingly set their drag too tight for it to function properly. In fact, I've known a few anglers who tighten their drag down with pliers! They give a bass no quarter, and feel that the best time to play with a lunker is after you have it in the boat.

Bassmen who prefer a very tight drag setting might want to consider the new Ambassadeur 5000D reel. Instead of a star drag, it has a knurled adjustment wheel located directly under the reel handle. The important point is that the drag works only when the forward pressure is relieved from the reel handle. To make use of the drag, the angler simply takes his hand off the reel handle. Then, the instant the handle is cranked forward, the reel shifts into direct drive and will not yield to a bass—unless the line breaks or the hooks fail.

As far as I know, the 5000D is the only baitcasting reel to have such a drag system, but it has been used on some spincast reels. A direct drive might be all right for experienced anglers, but I wouldn't recommend that anyone use it with a line lighter than 25-pound test, and I wouldn't recommend that the inexperienced angler use it at all. Many anglers, including some with years of experience, become quite excited when they tie into a lunker bass and are therefore likely to forget to relieve the pressure on the handle at critical points in the battle. Although the direct drive will help save some bass that would have tangled in treetops, the average angler is better off with a good star drag system.

The star drag mechanism on the better baitcasting reels works satisfactorily for bass fishing. Black bass are noted for an initial surge of brute strength and head-shaking tactics; they seldom make long, sustained runs like bonefish do, so that a drag mechanism binding from overheating is seldom a problem in bass fishing. But the washers in the star drag system must be kept well lubricated and in good condition. It's best to replace them every two years or so, and it's also a good idea to relieve the tension on the washers after each fishing trip. Keeping the washers under pressure for long periods of time can permanently compress them. But few anglers ever relieve the pressure on the washers, and I neglect it myself more often than not.

If you do relieve the tension on your drag after a fishing trip—and you should—be sure to tighten it down before you make another cast! Consider what can happen: Not long ago, I was taking a leisurely stroll along a canal near our house. After seeing a huge bass lazing about near a patch of grass, I headed home, not so leisurely now, and tied a 12-inch worm onto my baitcasting outfit. I didn't see the bass when I returned, but I cast out parallel to the line of grass. Two small bass, neither of them as long as the worm, came to investigate. They knocked the worm about and seemed to be fighting for it. Suddenly, in a swirl and a flash, the lunker came out of the grass bed and engulfed the worm. I reared back to set the hook, but only zipped line off the spool. Instead of "crossing his eyes," as bassmen like to say, I merely made the old lunker flinch before he spat the worm out. I was certainly more confused than the bass until I realized that I had not tightened the drag!

4

Spinning
and
Spincast Reels

ALL BAITCASTING REELS have revolving spools, whereas the spools on all spinning and spincast reels are fixed and do not revolve during the cast or during the retrieve. If you don't understand spinning reels, put a new spool of fishing line on the floor, grasp the end of the line between your fingers, and pull straight up. Notice that the line comes off the spool in coils while the spool itself remains stationary. This is the fixed-spool principle on which all spinning and spincast reels operate.

Because the spool itself does not turn, spinning reels are not as complicated as baitcasting reels. The mechanical tolerances aren't as critical either, so that spinning reels are not generally as expensive as baitcasting reels. They are easier to use, too, and backlashes—real backlashes—do not occur.

But the uncoiling line does cause some problems. In fact, the success of the spinning principle depends largely on having the right line. If a line is too limp, it will not spring off the reel properly and will create too much friction as it goes over the lip of the spool; if, on the other hand, the line is too stiff, it will spring off too quickly and will cause birds' nests. Monofilament line of the correct stiffness is ideal for spinning, and, in spite of the fact that spinning reels are quite old, the development of monofilament was the big breakthrough in widespread use of spinning tackle. Braided line can be used on spinning reels, but the smaller diameters are too limp for distance casting; and most braided lines simply cannot be used on spincast reels because they ball up under the face cup.

As was pointed out in the last chapter, a big disadvantage of the spinning principle is that the angler doesn't have enough control of the lure during the cast. He loses contact with it. If the angler sees that his lure is going to overshoot the mark and go into the bushes, he must stop it by engaging the bail or pushing the button; in either case, the lure is then likely to jerk back and splash down abruptly short of the target. With a revolving spool reel, by contrast, the angler can thumb the spool during the cast and sit the lure down gently on target. It is possible to "feather" a spinning line during the cast, but this method of control is not as positive as thumb contact with a revolving spool.

The spinning reel is, however, ideal for fishing light lures in open water. A good example is using spinning gear for catching schooling bass, where distance is often more important than pinpoint accuracy. In fact, one big advantage of spinning gear is that, if it is properly balanced and spooled, it permits the angler to cast light lures for long

Typical underslung, open-faced spinning reels.

distances. And open-faced underslung spinning reels have much more range than push-button, closed-faced spincast reels.

The trouble with spincast reels is that the coils of line must funnel through the small opening in the face cup. This creates a lot of friction and slows down the line. Another disadvantage is that the spools on typical spincast reels are too narrow, for reasons that will be discussed later. To be sure, there have been some improvements in spincast reels during recent years, but the only good thing I can say about the design as such is that spincast reels are so very easy to use. That's why they sell in larger numbers than all other reels combined. Some bass guides have to carry them along in their boats simply because their customers don't know how to use anything else. And, to be honest about it, spin-cast reels are capable of more distance than is normally required in bass fishing. Also, good spincast rigs are not only easy to use but also perform without trouble if they are properly spooled; for this reason, they may be a good choice for casting at night.

But accuracy is *the* important consideration in some types of bass fishing, so that neither spinning nor spincast reels are ideal for the sport. Yet, many bass anglers fish with nothing else, and almost all expert bassmen like to take a spinning rig along in addition to their baitcasting outfits. If for no other reason, it is a relief to pick up a properly balanced spinning rig off and on during the course of a long

A typical push-button, closed-faced spincast reel.

day's fishing. Some anglers like spinning reels because they are capable of retrieving a lure faster than baitcasting gear. This will be discussed below, along with other design considerations, features, and related topics:

Spools and spooling. One of the primary requirements for casting smoothly with a spinning outfit is that the spool must be full of line. If the spool is not full to within ⅛ inch of capacity, the line creates too much friction when it goes over the edge, and this limits both distance and accuracy. The less line on the spool, the greater the friction. But the spool shouldn't be *too* full. If it is, the line is apt to come off in tangled coils, or birds' nests, and sometimes the line becomes so tangled that part of it must be cut off and thrown away. Birds' nests are more likely to occur when line is too stiff for the diameter of the spool being used.

Ideally, one should spool with line within a certain range, which may or may not be specified by the manufacturer. As a general rule, a normal-sized freshwater spinning reel, with a spool of about 1¾ inches, will handle a line from 6 to 12 pounds test. But there is a good deal of difference between the stiffness of one brand of monofilament and another, so that a lot of leeway is possible if the angler chooses his line carefully.

In my opinion, most bass anglers tend to spool with line that is too heavy for normal-sized spinning rigs. If you want to fish with 20-pound monofilament, it is best to use it on a light saltwater spinning reel with a large spool. New, ultrasoft 20-pound monofilament may work fairly well on 1¾-inch spools in warm weather, but after long use some of the additives will leach out, the line will become wiry, and birds' nests are likely to occur.

The size and shape of the spool are important considerations in how well a spinning line casts. As stated in a brochure published by True Temper:

> To be practical, at least 80 percent of the rated line capacity of a reel should be usable for fishing. The spool should be open. That is, the span (distance between the flanges) must be as wide as possible with a large diameter, long spool hub.
>
> Such a spool allows all its rated line capacity to be wound relatively close to the outside diameter of the flange. When 40 to 60 percent of the line is removed from a short span, large diameter, small hub spool the casting performance is greatly reduced and drag builds up rapidly with no increase in retrieve power.

A wide span is especially important for distance casting, so that the spool will remain almost full during the cast. Most spincast reels, however, have spools with narrow spans, which, together with other design features, limit the distance obtainable. Also, light line doesn't work too well on narrow-span spools because it doesn't spring off properly when the spool becomes partly depleted during the cast. Heavier line and limited distance make the spincast reel unsuited for light lures, and most of them work best with lures from $\frac{3}{8}$ to $\frac{5}{8}$ ounce. Thus, the main advantages of spinning reels—distance, small line diameter, and the ability to cast light lures—are almost entirely lost on spincast reels.

Line guides. The spinning reel is probably the perfect design for distance casting with light lures simply because the spool and other parts remain stationary during the cast. But it is not the perfect retrieve mechanism. Far from it. First of all, the spool must oscillate during the retrieve so that the line will wind on smoothly, and the line itself must be picked up and wound onto the spool by some sort of post, roller, or line guide that revolves around the spool. The line must make a 90-degree turn at the line guide and must slide over the line guide (or metal post) before it is wound onto the spool.

The various bail and line guide devices work smoothly enough on most good spinning reels, but they all create friction and abrade the line to one degree or another. In my opinion, the worst sort of line guide is a small metal post, or pin, and those that cannot be replaced easily are especially bad. The next worst is a fixed line guide in the bail piece; some of these are replaceable, but some designs require that the entire bail be replaced. The best possible line guide—at least in theory —is a roller that turns during the retrieve. Rollers are usually available only on the most expensive reels, such as the Orvis line. I own some reels without roller guides, but I don't think I'll ever buy another one. A good roller guide is worth the extra money, and I, for one, would be willing to pay for a roller guide made with aluminum oxide sleeves. In any case, it is important to inspect a roller guide frequently to see that it is turning freely. It should be lubricated often, or according to the manufacturer's instructions, and it *must* be kept clean at all times.

If an angler doesn't have a roller guide on his spinning rig, the best he can do is inspect his line guide for wear. But microscopic pitting in tungsten carbide rollers or fixed guides may not be apparent to the naked eye, or even with the aid of a magnifying glass. The best bet is to replace them from time to time. A representative of a large reel company recently told me that they used stainless steel line guides instead of carbide, simply because a tiny crack or other imperfection in carbide (which is brittle stuff) can quickly ruin a line. He also told me that they were thinking seriously about using aluminum oxide, and I would like to see them proceed with it.

Generally, the line guides on spinning reels are better, both in design and in practice, than the metal posts used on spincast reels. Because of design problems, it is difficult to use a roller or any other line guide except a straight post. Most of the posts, or pins, used on spincast reels have a small diameter as compared to line guides on spinning reels. Also, the posts of some spincast reels can severely pinch a line against the face cup.

Retrieve factor. The average spinning reel has a retrieve ratio of about 3.8 to 1, and some high-speed reels go as high as 5 to 1. And the retrieve ratio itself isn't the whole story. Typically, spinning reels have spools with comparatively large diameters. The highly popular Mitchell 300 spinning reel, for example, has a spool diameter of about 1¾ inches, whereas the Ambassadeur 5000 baitcasting reel has a spool diameter of about 1½ inches. That extra quarter of an inch in diameter makes a lot of difference in the amount of line the reel hauls in for each turn of the handle. For example, the normal-sized Orvis 100S spinning reel (with a retrieve ratio of 4.8 to 1) hauls in about 30 inches of line per turn of the handle, whereas an Ambassadeur 5000 (with 4.8-to-1 replacement gears) hauls in only 21 or 22 inches of line per turn of the handle.

What all this boils down to is that the typical spinning reel is a good deal faster than the typical baitcasting reel. In fact, large spinning reels with wide spools haul in more line than would be possible with bait-casting gear, and some bass anglers achieve lightning fast retrieves by using large spinning reels on long rods. Called ripping, the trick is to raise the tip of the rod fast while simultaneously cranking away at the reel handle. Ripping can at times be effective in triggering bass to strike. The technique is not difficult, but true ripping can be achieved only with spinning reels with wide spools.

Drag. As far as I know, the drag systems on all the better spinning and spincast reels are adequate for bass fishing. I personally prefer a good multiwasher drag system, but the spring-type drag rings used on the old Mitchell 300 reels are smooth enough (for bass fishing) provided that they are kept in good shape. They should be lubricated according to the manufacturer's instructions, and the tension should always be relieved after a fishing trip. Long storage under pressure can warp, compress, or deform drag rings and washers.

Most spinning reel drags are adjusted on the spool frame itself, but this is not universal. The new Zebco Cardinal 4, for example, has a calibrated drag knob on the body of the reel. I've never noticed a star wheel drag on a spinning reel, but they are pretty much standard on most of the better spincast reels.

Replaceable spools. One of the most convenient features of some spinning reels is that the line spools can be removed and replaced in seconds. This feature makes it extremely easy to change from one line to another merely by snapping spools in and out, and the complete angler will have two or three spools for each reel.

Garcia and other firms sell their extra spools in a canister-type plastic box designed for a spool of certain size, and these boxes are great for storing spools and line. Tip: If you have several of these spool-and-canister sets, stick a piece of tape on the bottom and write the type and size of line on it; this will save time, avoid confusion, and prevent mistakes. It can also save a bass for you. Once, for example, my brother borrowed my spinning rig and lost a lunker, possibly because I gave him an old spool of line that I was saving for crappie fishing!

Under the headings above, I have discussed the basic spinning and spincast designs and problems. Here are some innovations and new designs, together with a couple of gadgets for using on spinning reels:

Uni-Spin. True Temper has come up with a neat push-button, underslung, open-faced spinning reel, available in two sizes for light and heavy fishing. Since the push button extends up through the rod handle, one must purchase the whole outfit as a set. (The rod is a two-piece design, and tips are available in light, medium, and heavy actions.) Although I personally prefer a regular spinning outfit, many other anglers may like the push-button release. My nephew, for example, fished with my Uni-Spin 66 for several weeks and thinks it's the greatest.

The Uni-Spin has a unique drag system. On most other spinning or spincast reels, the spool itself turns when the drag slips. If you crank the handle while the drag is slipping, line twist will occur. This twist is multiplied by the retrieve ratio of the reel, and I've seen fishermen completely ruin a line by cranking away while hooked into a big fish, or a stump. This kind of line twist is not possible with the Uni-Spin drag system, which allows the cup—not the spool—to revolve when the drag

is slipping. Another feature of the Uni-Spin is that the actual drag setting remains constant no matter how much line is left on the spool.

Closed-face underslung reels. A few closed-face reels are designed
to be used on regular spinning rods instead of on spincast or ordinary
baitcasting rods. The casting technique is similar to that of regular
spinning reels in that the angler releases the line with his finger.
Frankly, I can see little advantage to closed-face underslung reels, and
there is a big disadvantage in that the line has to funnel through the
opening in the face cup, thereby causing friction and reducing distance.

The Johnson Reel people advertise their Century and Citation models
as usable on either spinning or casting rods—and even on fly rods.
Actually, almost any spincast reel can be used as an underslung reel,
except that the handle has to be turned backward to retrieve a lure. If
I understand the Johnson literature correctly, their Century or Citation
reels have reversible handle drives and flop-over spools.

Because I have good underslung spinning reels, I haven't fished with
spincast reels on spinning rods. But I did, for the heck of it, put a spincast reel on an 8½-foot fly rod, and with this outlandish rig I threw
a lure out of sight. Not long ago I noticed a guy fishing with a Zebco
One mounted on a long two-handed spinning rod, and he was getting a
lot of distance with it. I have also read an article or two in outdoor
magazines about people using spincast reels on fly rods, reportedly with
great success. If I remember correctly, the main character in one such
article claimed that he used the rig because it was so accurate. I won't
argue with that here, but I do suggest that the long, slow action of the
fly rod would indeed make the spincast reels more accurate than the
typical ultra-fast rods that most spincasters use. The slower the rod, the
less critical the push-button timing must be.

Retractable spool shields. The French-made Martin Bretton 600
spinning reels feature a retractable spool shield. In effect, this design
eliminates the troublesome pickup bail and offers the advantage of a
protective spool shield. The spool shield retracts before the cast is made,
thereby eliminating the friction associated with closed-face spinning
or spincast reels. On the retrieve, a carbide pin picks up the line and
winds it onto the spool when the reel handle is turned. It's a neat design; the reel is easier to use than a regular spinning model, and it has
more range than spincast models. The only objection that I have is to
the carbide pin; I would prefer some sort of roller guide.

Direct drive. A few spincast reels, such as the Johnson Sabra, offer the angler the option of a drag system or a direct drive. While the angler is turning the reel handle or holding it steady, the reel is in direct drive and will not give out line; but when the angler removes his hand from the reel handle (or turns it backward slightly), a drag system engages so that a fish can strip off line.

Although the design has merits, and a direct drive may come in handy in a "stop it now or never" situation, I have come to the conclusion that the average angler, who is most likely to be using spincast gear in the first place, will often, through excitement, use the direct drive when it isn't desirable to do so. In short, I think the direct drive will cost the average angler more lunkers than it will save him, especially if he has spooled up with anything less than 20-pound line. The direct drive is, however, a worthwhile feature for the seasoned angler, or for the newcomer who uses his head and keeps his cool.

Triggers. Gudebrod and possibly other firms offer little thumb-operated devices that hold and release line for underslung spinning reels. Without such a device, the angler must pick up the line with his index finger, and then release it on the cast. Personally, I believe that the finger release is the best system for spinning reels, and I don't think any sort of trigger is needed unless the angler is missing an index finger. But Gudebrod, who has a good name for quality products, says that the device increases both distance and accuracy. I don't see how, but any angler who has trouble with the usual finger release should certainly look into the devices. In addition to the add-on devices (which fit neatly onto the rod just above the reel bail), a few reels are being manufactured with some such gadget attached to them.

Manual pickup. In contrast to push-button-inclined anglers who install triggers on spinning rigs, some of the purists prefer a reel without even a bail. At the end of the cast and just before starting the retrieve, the angler picks up the line with his finger and flips it over a line guide or roller on the revolving cup. The process is not really complicated, and it becomes a matter of habit after a while. A manual reel is lighter, neater, and more trouble-free than those with bail mechanisms. In fact, most of the problems I have had with spinning reels have been with the bail mechanism.

A few reels, mostly ultralight models, are made without a bail, and some manufacturers market kits to convert their regular bail pickup reels to manual. In my opinion, a manual pickup reel with a good roller line guide is the ultimate spinning rig for reducing line abrasion to a minimum and for providing trouble-free operation. Good ones are a joy to use, too.

Interchangeable handles. Although many reputable manufacturers of spinning reels and spincast reels offer models for both right- and left-handed anglers, retailers seldom stock reels for left-handers because they don't sell many of them. Some of the newer reels have detachable handles that can be used on either side of the reel. This is a good feature not only for left-handers but also for manufacturers and retailers because it simplifies ordering, stocking, and manufacture.

Spooler. Any angler who has trouble putting new monofilament line on spinning and spincast reels should consider an inexpensive gadget made by Featherweight Products. It fits onto the front of the reel, will work with either $\frac{1}{4}$-pound bulk spools or with two joined 100-yard spools, and, if properly used, will help prevent line twist.

The term "ultralight" is a relative one, but even so, most bass anglers stretch its meaning out of all bounds. An 8-pound line on a $1\frac{3}{4}$-inch spool is not ultralight; it is, in fact, the normal line for use on a normal-sized freshwater spinning reel, no matter how light it might seem to pluggers accustomed to 25-pound line and worm rods. A true ultralight reel has a much smaller spool and carries smaller line. The tiny Orvis 50A, for example, was designed for 2-pound line; although it will work with 4- or even 6-pound line, 8-pound stuff won't spool or cast properly and tends to come off in coils, causing birds' nests. Although 6-pound line will work on tiny reels, I would say that anything over 4-pound is not ultralight.

True ultralight gear is designed to cast $\frac{1}{8}$ and $\frac{1}{16}$ ounce lures with 4-pound and 2-pound line (or 3-pound, if you can find it). Because bass, especially largemouth, will usually take larger baits, and because the bass shows a marked preference for cover and underwater structure, the 2- and 4-pound lines are not practical for most bass fishing. They lose too many fish and break off too many lures. To be sure, properly balanced ultralight gear is a pleasure to use and will catch a lot of bass, but the bass angler really needs a line heavy enough to pull lures free from snags. I might add that if the bass angler doesn't hang his lure frequently, he is not fishing where the bass are most likely to be.

There are times, however, when small-diameter lines seem to make a lot of difference in bass fishing, especially in gin-clear lakes and small streams. (And smallmouth bass will at times show a preference for tiny lures.) For this reason many expert bass anglers go down to 6-

pound line. And 6-pound line *in excellent condition* is heavy enough to land a lunker bass if you can keep it out of treetops.

My conclusion is that the complete bassman ought to take along some 6-pound line, but that he shouldn't use it if the bass will hit heavier stuff. By the way, there's nothing wrong with using 6-pound line on a baitcasting outfit, or with using a 6-pound leader on heavier line. Whatever gear is used for fishing a light or ultralight line, it had better be kept in working condition and should be of top quality. Pay particular attention to rod guides and tips, line guides, and drag mechanisms.

I don't recommend a line smaller than 6-pound test for the average bass angler, but if you do decide to purchase an ultralight spinning rig, give some thought to the matter before selecting a "matched" rod and reel. Most rods made for ultralight reels are not long enough to cast $\frac{1}{16}$-ounce lures. Although short rods may *look* better with small reels— and far too much tackle is in fact sold on looks instead of performance —they simply will not cast ultralight lures. In my opinion, an ultralight rod should be at least 6 feet long and should have a soft, full-flex action. But such a rod should not be used with large lures or with plastic worms because it isn't stiff enough to set large hooks properly.

5

Fishing Lines

Some trout anglers measure the diameter of their tippets with precision micrometers and may think in terms of thousandths of an inch instead of in terms of the more common pound-test ratings. Although there is considerable difference in the comparative diameters of lines of various manufacture, the pound-test rating is usually close enough for practical bass fishing. Because the bass doesn't feed extensively on minute insects, it is probably not as sharp-eyed as the trout. But the bass has, I've read, been rated by some biologists as the smartest of all freshwater sport fish. They aren't blind, either, so that, in short, the visibility of the fishing line *is* an important consideration in bass fishing.

It is impossible for the bass angler to have a perfect line for all occasions. When fishing in submerged timber in a clear lake, for example, an 8-pound line will usually get more strikes than a 25-pound line, but the lighter line will cause the angler to lose more bass and lures in the treetops. The general rule of thumb among bassmen is to use the heaviest line that they can get away with. On a particular day on a certain lake, for example, the expert might start with a 25-pound line. If he fails to catch bass from likely holding or feeding areas, he'll go down to 17-pound. Then to 10-pound. Sometimes even to 6-pound. The complete bass angler will, of course, have several rods and reels spooled

This angler used a strong monofilament line to land this Toledo Bend lunker bass.

with different weights of line. Those who can't afford many rigs, or who don't like to switch from one to the other, would do well to have a reel with interchangeable spools. If an angler prefers to fish with one weight of line all the time, then he must make a choice. Personally, I would choose a 17-pound monofilament.

As discussed later in this chapter, one solution to this problem is to use leaders on a basic line. This will, of course, allow the angler to change the diameter on the terminal end of his rig, but unfortunately the terminal end isn't the only consideration.

It is impossible to get either distance or accuracy with a light lure tied to a heavy line, either with baitcasting or with spinning rigs. A heavy line with a large diameter has more air resistance than a light line. Too much air resistance slows down a lure and makes it fall short of the mark. It also tends to cause backlashes and birds' nests. In addition, the sheer weight of a line will slow the lure down. Obviously, one could not cast a $\frac{1}{2}$-ounce lure with a plow line. Nor can he cast a $\frac{3}{16}$-ounce lure with a 25-pound line. It follows that a light line always casts better than a heavy one (except when fishing with fly-fishing gear). But as a practical matter, casting line can't be *too* light because the last few inches of the line, between rod tip and lure, really catch hell during a cast; a light line is likely to snap and send the lure flying off. Purely from a *casting* viewpoint, the following table is a rough guide to matching modern lines and lures:

Weight of Lure (ounces)	Test Weight of Line (pounds)
$\frac{1}{4}$	8 to 10
$\frac{3}{8}$	10 to 12
$\frac{1}{2}$	12 to 14
$\frac{5}{8}$	14 to 15
$\frac{3}{4}$	14 to 17

But most bassmen—who are more concerned with fishing than with casting as such—use heavier line, and in all fairness I must say that a $\frac{5}{8}$-ounce lure casts nicely with a good 20- or 25-pound line. On the other hand, anglers who have problems in casting $\frac{1}{4}$-ounce lures with a baitcasting rig will be pleasantly surprised if they try an 8-pound line and a light, slow rod of suitable length (6 or 6$\frac{1}{2}$ feet).

Another point to consider when choosing a line is the depth at which the angler wants a particular lure to run. This is especially important with floating/diving lures such as the Hellbender and the Big-O. The lighter the line, the deeper the lure goes at a given rate of retrieve. Indeed, some savvy bassmen often change line just to make a diving plug go deeper. The reason for this is that a large line has more water resistance than a smaller line, and tends to rise on the retrieve.

Still another good point to consider is that the stiffness of the line has an influence on the action of some lures. This is especially true of monofilament. A stiff 25-pound monofilament will kill the action of a Rapala or a Johnson Silver Minnow. One solution to this problem is to put a split ring in the lure eyelet, which serves as a sort of universal joint between line and lure. Another solution is to use some sort of loop knot in the end of the line, but I've never seen a loop knot that didn't drastically reduce the line's strength or slip down when pressure is applied. Some slipknots are strong enough, but who wants to retie the loop every time he catches a bass or hangs up on a tree limb? I therefore recommend the split ring instead of loop knots.

Finally, the weight or size of a line can have an adverse influence on the feel of a lure, and the resistance caused by a heavy line can decrease the angler's chances of detecting a bump on a plastic worm or free-falling lure when he's jigging, counting down, or yo-yoing.

Monofilament is by far the most popular fishing line on the market today. It is almost universally used on spinning and spincast gear, and most bass anglers even spool it on baitcasting reels. Although monofilament is getting better and better, and new imports such as Nylorfi from France and Maxima from West Germany together with many American-made brands give the angler a wide choice, the fact remains that the perfect monofilament doesn't yet exist. And probably never will.

Monofilament has several interrelated properties—visibility, strength, knot strength, stretch, impact resistance, softness, limpness—and often improvements in one property are at the expense of another. For example, it is difficult to make a particular line more limp without also giving it more stretch, so that advertising claims of "very low stretch" and "ultra limp" for the same line are suspect.

I discussed the various properties of monofilament in my *Fishing for Bass,* and the text below is based on that book:

Strength-to-diameter ratio. The strength of a line is expressed in the number of pounds required to break it; a 20-pound line will support at least 20 pounds of weight without breaking. But the pound test published on the line's label isn't the whole story. Most line makers rate their lines a bit lower than the actual laboratory tests indicate. Another point to remember is that a line is stronger when dry than when wet. A line will slowly absorb a good deal of moisture from the air or from the water, and a fully saturated line loses about 10 to 15 percent of its strength.

Other characteristics being equal, a 20-pound line with a diameter of 0.019 inch is, in my opinion, better than one with a diameter of 0.023 inch. The line with the smaller diameter will usually cast better, will be less visible to the fish, and will permit some lures with built-in action to perform better. On the other hand, the line with the smaller diameter will be more likely to fail because of nicks or abrasion; and for this reason some bassmen actually prefer a larger line! In any case, strength-to-diameter ratios certainly aren't the only criteria for selecting a monofilament fishing line.

Stretch. The more a line stretches when one jerks on the rod, the less energy or pull there is to set the hook. In other words, a line can act rather like a shock absorber. A degree of stretch is highly desirable to cushion the sudden jolt of a large fish hitting close to the boat, but most monofilament lines have far too much stretch instead of not enough.

I never did realize just how much some brands of monofilament stretch until I took a roll dove hunting. Actually, I was trying to get a striking photograph to illustrate an article I had written about dove hunting. I wanted a bird between the camera and the hunter so that it would be big in the picture. To get the shot, I drove a stake into the ground and mounted the camera on it. Then I put a screw-eye into the stake and ran an 8-pound monofilament line through it. One end of the line was tied to the camera shutter release lever, and the other was tied to my boot. The idea was that when a dove flew between me and the camera, I could trip the shutter by pulling on the line. But when making a test shot, I was awfully surprised to find that the monofilament stretched too much to trip the shutter! Of course, the line would have tripped the shutter if I could have pulled it out far enough, but the span of my foot swing just wouldn't do the trick. I finally got my photograph, but this experience taught me more about fishing than about photography. If that line wouldn't trip a camera's shutter, I realized, it would be very difficult to set a large hook with it.

Softness. Some monofilament lines are more limp or more flexible than others. Generally, softness is a highly desirable quality in a line. A soft line is easier to cast and results in better action on some types of lures. A wiry line inhibits lure action and tends to coil excessively after it has been put on a spool, causing birds' nests during the cast. On the other hand, a line can be too limp for use on spinning and spincast reels; if it is too limp, it will not spring off the spool correctly and may ball up under closed-face reels. A limp line also tends to slap the rod more, which reduces an angler's casting distance because of friction. Generally, a very soft monofilament will also have too much stretch.

One obvious way to reduce or increase softness is to put on a lighter or a heavier line. A 10-pound line will be more limp than a 20-pound line. But there is also quite a lot of difference in softness between various brands of monofilament of the same test strength. A good deal also depends on whether the line is wet or dry, new or old. A wet line is softer than a dry line, and a new line is often softer than an old one that has been used extensively. In time, water will leach out the additives that the manufacturer uses to make a line soft.

Knot strength. When tying monofilament line to a hook or plug eyelet, or to another line, it is very important that you use the proper knot and tie it correctly. But some monofilament lines do have better knot strength than others. A very soft, highly elastic line, for example, compresses under pressure and tends to slip or fail. It is also difficult to draw a knot down properly with limp monofilament.

Visibility. Monofilament line is not entirely invisible to bass, but it is less visible than braided line. Some monofilament is clear, while others are tinted with one color or another. I've never been able to determine whether or not bass can tell any difference between clear or tinted line, and, frankly, I place more importance on diameter. Even so, I don't believe that visibility is as important when fishing fast-moving lures like the Weed Wing as when fishing slow-moving baits like the plastic worm.

For some kinds of fishing, I like to use a line that *I* can see (and which, I hope, the bass can't see). I often use a line as a visual indicator because any twitch or change in line movement can mean that a bass has taken the lure. (Instead of striking a lure as is commonly believed, the bass usually engulfs it by opening its gills and sucking water and bait into its huge mouth, so that many strikes on still or free-falling baits are very gentle.) I can see a line twitch better when I use good polarized sunglasses, but some lines are indeed more visible to me than others. Du Pont's fluorescent Stren line is generally considered to be more visible to the angler than are most other brands.

Abrasion resistance. Normal fishing will cause abrasion to one degree or another. Pulling the line through rod tips and guides, over brush in the water, or bumping it along the bottom all cause abrasion. During the casting process, the last few inches of line really catch hell, what with the lure being stopped and snapped forward at the end of the backcast. Fighting a bass will often abrade the last few inches of line drastically. It always pays to cut off a few inches of line after catching a fish or when changing lures.

Although some degree of abrasion cannot be avoided, it can be held to a minimum by careful inspection of the line and tackle. Pay particular attention to rod guides and tips, and to the line guides or rollers on spinning and spincast reels. Also inspect lure and hook eyelets. A worn or rusty eyelet can cause severe line abrasion when the knot is drawn down tight.

At best, abrasion is microscopic; at worst, it falls into the category of nicks and gouges. Nicks cause stress concentration, which means that the line's strength is drastically reduced. Incidentally, it is easier to nick or abrade stiff monofilament than soft. The reason is that soft monofilament is more flexible and elastic. On the other hand, monofilament that has been in the water for several hours may lose as much as 50 percent of its abrasion resistance, and tests indicate that the line never recovers all of its abrasion resistance once it has become fully saturated.

Impact strength. One cause of line failure occurs when an angler sets the hook very hard into a large bass. Although impact failure sometimes occurs close to the boat, a more common cause is slack line, so that the full force of the angler's jerk hits suddenly. Plastic-worm fishermen using low-stretch line and stiff worm rods should be especially conscious of impact and should not set the hook until all the slack is out of the line.

Note that a line's impact strength is lower than its tensile strength. Generally, lines with high stretch are less likely to break from impact. And the more line that is out, the less the danger of impact failure.

A bonefish guide in the Florida Keys once told me that he changed line on his reels every time he took a client out fishing, and I'm sure that most of the bass tournament fishermen also respool each day. It's my experience that any monofilament line should be replaced often, but this can be expensive. Some anglers who change often buy inexpensive line. I don't recommend cheap line, but I personally think that it is indeed better to buy inferior line and change it frequently than to buy expensive line and leave it on too long. The best bet is to buy premium line in bulk spools.

Most of the monofilament sold in this country comes on 100-yard spools, or on two connecting 100-yard spools. One problem, in addition to cost, is that a 100-yard spool may not be enough to fill one's reel— and 200 yards may be too much. It's a good deal easier to fill a reel to capacity by using a bulk spool. Some of the better-known lines, such as Stren and Trilene XL, can be bought in ¼-pound spools, and it is possible to buy even larger spools if you can find a dealer who stocks them. Stren, for example, can be obtained in 2,400-yard spools. Anyhow, the larger the spool, the greater the savings.

Another way to economize on line is to use either a reel arbor or backing line, so that all the spool doesn't have to be filled with new line. Also, interchangeable spools of different line capacity are available for some of the better reels. I prefer backing line on spinning reels instead of short-capacity spools; but an arbor seems to be the better choice for baitcasting reels, especially if the angler uses light lures. When using heavier lures on a casting outfit, I really prefer to have the backing line, just in case I need it. Generally, however, 50 yards of line is all one needs for bass fishing. An exception would be with the use of ultralight tackle and line in the 4-pound class.

If you do not fish often and leave line on a reel for long periods, keep it out of sunlight or fluorescent light, either of which can considerably degrade a line. (Strong sunlight is much worse than fluorescent light.) If the line is protected from light, however, it can be stored dry for a number of years without any measurable deterioration.

There are several good knots for tying hooks and lures to monofilament, but I recommend the standard improved clinch knot for this purpose. With line smaller than 30-pound test, it is important that the end line be wrapped five turns. More turns just make it more difficult to draw the knot down properly, and fewer turns can reduce the knot strength drastically. Some anglers double the line before tying the clinch knot, and others wrap the line around the eyelet twice. In my opinion and experience, neither procedure increases knot strength, and both make it more difficult to tie the knot and draw it down properly.

It is important that the clinch knot be tied perfectly and drawn down with a smooth, steady pressure. Lubricating the knot with water or saliva before drawing it down tight will help. Personally, I hold the lure (or hook) in my left hand, the line in my right, and the loose end between my teeth. Then I apply pressure from three directions simultaneously.

I once fished with a fellow who didn't know how to draw a mono-filament knot down properly, and for his own good I presumed to tell him so. He replied that he had been tying fishing knots when I was still wet behind the ears. A few casts later, he had a "strike" on a red plastic worm and let the fish run. When he finally set the hook, the line went slack and he reeled in minus his red worm. "Broke my line," he said. "What a bass!"

I didn't say anything, but I knew from the way the end of his line was kinked that the knot had slipped. While he was tying on another worm, a 10-inch bass jumped up within four feet of the boat, violently shaking an 8-inch worm. It was a red worm.

The trouble was that this fellow wasn't drawing the knot down tight enough. After that experience, he started leaving about ½ inch of end line sticking out from his knots. This may help sometimes, but not always. Once a knot starts slipping, it may continue to slip until the end works through. One trick that some anglers use is to touch a cigarette or match flame to the end of the line, which melts the nylon into a little ball, but I don't think this is necessary when using the improved clinch knot if it is tied properly. Personally, I always clip my knots *very* close with nail clippers, and I seldom have a slippage problem.

I don't have any data and haven't run any tests, but I believe that there is an ideal relation, or proportion, between the diameter of a monofilament line and the diameter of the hook or plug eyelet. A small line tied to a large eyelet tends to slip. An example would be a 4-pound line tied to a 5/0 hook. At the other extreme, a large line tied to a small eyelet is likely to break at far below its rated pound test. An example would be a 25-pound line tied to a small-diameter wire eyelet in a homemade balsa plug. I don't know whether the wire eyelet cuts into the line or whether it causes a severe bending and stress concentration at the outer bend of the line. In any case, I usually put a split ring in a wire eyelet.

Finally, I want to emphasize that a knot tied at the beginning of a fishing trip should be tested for slippage after the line has soaked up some water. The knot should also be tested after long use, but, of course, the experienced angler will routinely cut off the end of the line and retie from time to time.

Anyone who has trouble casting with modern baitcasting reels should consider using braided lines instead of monofilament. Purely from a casting viewpoint, braided line is the sensible choice for *any* baitcasting reel and is really the *only* practical choice for baitcasting reels that aren't free-spooling. But one braided line may not be as good as another. Generally, the softer the line, the better it casts—and some braided lines are too stiff for baitcasting reels, either because of the manufacturing process and materials or because of waterproofing and other additives.

Hard-braided lines are manufactured by lightly weaving threads over a solid core. Soft-braided lines are not woven around a core, and the weave is rather loose, so that the line itself is limp and tends to flatten on the reel spool. (Soft-braided lines are sometimes called square-braid or solid-braid, and hard-braided lines are sometimes called round- or oval-braids, depending on the shape of the core.) Although soft-braided line casts better than hard, it doesn't last as long.

Hard- and soft-braided lines are available in several materials, and sometimes it is difficult to tell exactly what the material is. Cortland's Micron line is described in their catalog as a "remarkable new synthetic fibre," but they don't say exactly what the material is. (Good stuff, whatever.) Some firms offer what is called "braided monofilament," which is simply a line made by braiding together about 8 strands of small monofilament. I used a Pflueger braided monofilament for about a year, and I found that it works very nicely on a baitcasting reel. It is limp enough and doesn't have a coil memory like regular monofilament has. Braided monofilament does, however, haul in a lot of water and in my opinion would be undesirable in cold weather or when plugging at night. It also seems to be heavier than braided lines of similar pound test.

Apart from braided monofilament and cryptic "synthetic fibres," braided lines are usually classified as follows:

Dacron. Braided dacron of good manufacture is an excellent choice for most baitcasting applications, and for trolling. It is almost immune to deterioration caused by exposure to sunlight, and it is also highly resistant to rot and mildew. It has a small diameter and spools nicely on baitcasting reels. One whopping advantage of dacron is that it has low stretch. Here's part of a press release prepared for a great champion of dacron, Gudebrod Brothers Silk Company:

> To find the overall stretch comparison of dacron vs. monofilament, we collected several 20-pound test monofilament lines of both premium and inexpensive quality, tied 3-foot lengths of it and our 20-pound dacron to a rack, and stretched them until they broke. The dacron stretched in a range of 8 to 14 percent before

breaking—and the monofilament stretched from 20 to 33 percent. It was interesting to note that the wide cost range of the monofilament seemed to have no bearing at all on how much they stretched.

A line was tied to a popular deep diving bass plug and pressure was applied until one hook (of a treble) was driven to the depth of the barb in the end grain of a block of balsa. The average pressure required was 5 pounds by use of a hand scale found in hardware stores. We will use this 5 pound figure for our comparisons.

Next, 12-inch lengths of monofilament and dacron were stretched until 5 pounds of pressure was applied. The 12 inches of monofilament stretched to 13 inches before the 5 pounds of pressure was reached. The 12 inches of dacron stretched to 12.5 inches before the 5 pounds of pressure was reached.

One might ask what difference can half an inch in a foot make? The answer is none—until you try to strike a bass 30 yards away where that difference grows to 4½ feet. At 30 yards, a fisherman using monofilament must take up 8.1 feet of line in order to apply the 5 pounds of pressure needed to set the hook, whereas the fisherman using dacron must take up only 3.6 feet of line before he hits home.

Furthermore, if the fisherman uses a popular model 5½-foot casting rod, holds it in the horizontal position during the retrieve, and then moves it to a vertical position to make the strike, he has only a possible 8½ foot striking arc distance in which to move the rod, as shown in Figure A.

In Figure B, we see that 5 pounds of pressure on the average 5½ foot casting rod causes the rod to bend, leaving only a possible striking arc of 5 feet. As shown in Figure C, the fisherman using monofilament would have to move the rod more than 90 degrees in order to apply 5 pounds of pressure.

In Figure D, we show the more likely position of the rod during the retrieve, which is a little above the horizontal, and see that to set the 5 pounds of pressure with monofilament requires that the rod be pulled way behind the head and shoulders in order to recover the 8 feet of line whereas dacron applies the pressure before or near the vertical.

The more the rod is held towards the vertical during the retrieve, the less opportunity to take up the line stretch with your upward rod sweep in order to gain that 5 pounds of pressure. Therefore, it stands to reason that the less distance you have to move the rod tip, the more likely you are to set the hook. That distance is reduced by more than half when using dacron line.

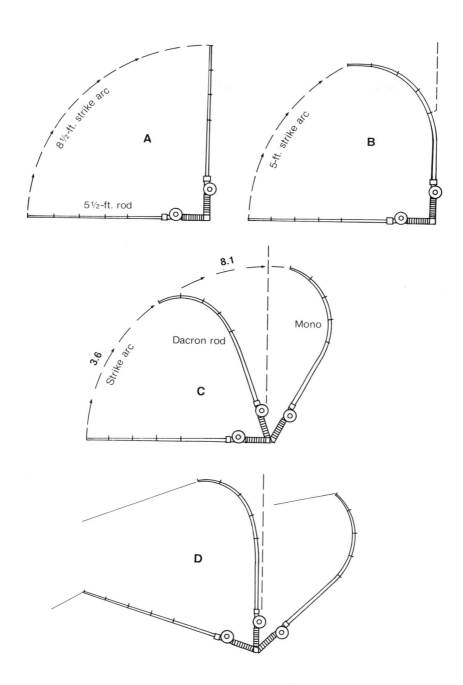

A

8½-ft. strike arc

5½-ft. rod

B

5-ft. strike arc

C

8.1

3.6

Strike arc

Dacron rod

Mono

D

In addition to its hook-setting properties, a low-stretch line is highly desirable on other counts. It is, for one thing, more sensitive to a strike —which can be very important in bass fishing, especially when using fall baits or slowly fished plastic worms.

Although I am personally sold on dacron fishing line, I must point out that the arc-length figures Gudebrod used are based on a rod-to-lure distance of 30 yards. That's 90 feet, and most bass anglers don't fish that far out. Moreover, I think it makes a lot of difference in *how* pressure is applied when setting a hook; a jerk is more effective than a slow, steady pull. Another point that I want to make is that any low-stretch line doesn't have the shock absorbing qualities of a high-stretch line. Low-stretch line, a stiff worm rod, and a tight drag could possibly cause you to lose a lunker bass, especially at close quarters. Still another disadvantage is that dacron is more visible than monofilament. But I think that the advantages—low stretch and casting ease—outweigh the disadvantages, and that you can overcome the visibility problem by using a monofilament leader (discussed later in this chapter).

Braided nylon. A braided nylon line of good quality works much better than monofilament on baitcasting reels. It spools better and casts easier. Typically, it has less stretch than monofilament but more than dacron. There is, of course, a wide range of stretch between one brand of line and another brand, but here's a rule-of-thumb stretch factor guide:

Monofilament	Braided Nylon	Dacron
20%	15%	10%

Braided nylon is not as impervious to sunlight as dacron, but it is a great improvement over the old silk lines in that it is stronger, wears better, and doesn't rot as easily.

Although dacron may be better than braided nylon for trolling and for deep-water fishing, nylon is my choice for fishing surface lures because it floats better. Some nylon lines, such as Cortland's Heart-o-Gold, are made primarily for surface fishing.

Silk and linen. Braided silk line is seldom seen today, but it is still available. The big advantage of silk as a fishing line is that it has very little stretch. The big disadvantage is that it rots and must be dried after each fishing trip.

Soft-braided (untreated and nonwaterproofed) silk is one of the finest *casting* lines made, but it is generally unsuited for bass fishing because it doesn't wear well. It is, however, an excellent choice for tournament casting.

About 20 or 30 years ago, linen line was popular with some anglers, but today it is manufactured on a very limited basis. Linen line is much stronger when wet than when dry, so that many anglers soaked their line before fishing with it. The main advantage of linen was that it had very low stretch.

The question of monofilament versus braided line is an interesting one, but with me it has become almost academic as far as fishing for bass is concerned. It's monofilament for spinning; braided for baitcasting. The baitcaster can, however, have the best of both lines simply by using a short monofilament leader on braided line. I have done just that for the past year, and I think that more bassmen ought to try it. Of course, the idea isn't my personal flash of brilliance, but I'll bet that less than 5 percent of bass anglers use leaders unless they happen to be fishing with a fly rod.

On a normal baitcasting outfit balanced for $\frac{5}{8}$-ounce lures, I use a 15- or 20-pound dacron line and a 5-foot leader. (The leader should not be too long because it would be undesirable for the knot to wind up past the line guide on the reel.) The size of the leader I use depends in large measure on where I am fishing, the amount of cover, and the water clarity. In very clear water, I'll use 10- or 12-pound leaders, but in murky water (or in heavy cover) I'll go up to 20-pound leaders. I also tend to use heavier leaders when I am fishing fast-moving lures.

The common blood knot is not ideal for tying a monofilament leader to a dacron casting line, so that the bassman will do well to master the intricacies of the double nail knot. This knot has excellent strength because the lines do not cut into each other or into themselves. The knot also goes smoothly through rod guides and tip if it is tied properly and trimmed closely.

One big advantage to using leaders is that the angler doesn't inch away at his main line each time he changes lures. It is easy to waste several yards of line during a day's fishing if one changes lures often. Besides, the last two feet of a line should be cut off from time to time because of the beating it takes during casting, fighting fish, and pulling a lure through cover. When using a leader, the angler simply ties on a new one when the old one gets short, so that the main line is saved.

Conserving the main line not only saves money but also results in easier casting simply because the spool stays full much longer.

Whatever kind of line the bassman chooses, he should take precautions to dispose of it properly. Monofilament as well as modern braided lines are not quick to decompose and should never be thrown into the water or left on the bank of lake or stream. Fishing lines—and especially monofilament—can cut the grease seal in outboard motors and can cut the watertight seal in electric motors. I personally have had an electric motor ruined because some careless angler left monofilament in the water. If you do tangle your props in fishing line, remove it immediately. The more it twists and binds around the shaft, the more likely it will be to cut a seal.

Fishing lines have also killed thousands of birds. In New York State, a pathology project revealed that about 6 percent of the dead birds found were entangled in monofilament.

Clearly, the bass angler should not discard fishing line carelessly. Either burn it or bury it—or at least cut it up into short pieces before throwing it into the water.

6

Lures
and
Terminal Tackle

DON'T TELL MY WIFE, but I own well over a thousand dollars' worth of bass lures. In fact, I have so many plugs and spoons and bass bugs and spinnerbaits and plastic worms that I can't find what I want in my tackle box, and can't remember which lures are in which box. Sometimes I think that I would fare better, and might even catch more bass, if I would weed out all but a dozen or so favorites. If I did, I would end up with a highly personal selection—lures that I like and understand, lures that do what I want them to do, lures that cast nicely on my favorite rod and reel, lures that I have confidence in, lures that I like to fish. In short, my dozen would be different from another man's. But I'm not about to throw a lure away (unless it is a rattler that doesn't rattle or a spinner that doesn't spin), and my lure collection is likely to get even bigger. Like most other bass anglers, I keep looking for the magic lure and keep buying whatever is hot, or said to be hot, at the moment.

It's true that some lures are better than others some of the time, and that no lure is better than the rest all of the time, so that a variety of lures will help the expert angler catch more bass. But I'm not sure that the average angler, who might fish only once a week or so, needs 200 lures. He would be better off to learn to use a dozen correctly. Of course, people like me who write about fishing need at least 200 lures, not for fishing, you understand, but for testing purposes. . . .

During the past few years, I have thrown a lot of lures in the clear waters of Lake Weir, in Central Florida. (I fish in other places, but I happen to live on an island in Lake Weir, which makes it a convenient place in which to test lures.) I like to cast lures off my boat dock and study their wiggle at various retrieves, and I like to bounce them and hop them along a sandy beach to see how they behave when bumping bottom. I think that all anglers would benefit from this sort of experimentation and observation, and that it should be done when one isn't really fishing. A swimming pool is an ideal place.

Although I would certainly take a lot of lures along on a trip to another lake, some of my most successful short outings here on Lake Weir have been when I took out one good lure and stuck with it. Last spring, for example, I devised what I consider to be the greatest bass catcher of all time—at least for *me*, in spring, on Lake Weir. (More about this secret weapon later.) I caught an awful lot of bass on it in and around some lily pads across the way from my house. Then, one day, I couldn't get a strike. The bass weren't feeding? They wanted a different lure? A different color? No. The bass weren't there. For some reason known only to the bass, they had moved out. I found them 200 yards away, in similar cover.

Although some lures are undoubtedly better than others at certain times, the plain truth is that most bass lures will catch bass if they are fished correctly and with confidence. Of course, it would be a mistake to fish top-water plugs when the bass are 20 feet deep, and it would be a mistake to fish a fast-moving sputterbuzzer bait in very cold water when the metabolism of the bass is low. But the expert angler who knows the ways and habits of bass can take two lures and outfish the mediocre angler with a hundred lures in his tackle box. Just the other day, someone was ribbing one of my neighbors about not catching any bass, saying that he ought to go out with me for a few lessons. The guy replied that he could catch bass too if he had as many plugs and lures as I have. Maybe—but not necessarily. The guy usually fishes with plastic worms, and if he doesn't score with these things, all the hardware in my tackle boxes wouldn't help him.

I am not going into great detail here about particular lures because such a discussion would lead to fishing tactics and techniques, which are not within the subject of this book. (I devoted several chapters and many pages of my book *Fishing for Bass* to all manner of lures and how to fish them.) Instead, I would like to discuss some broad classes of lures, with emphasis on quality and performance, together with some topics and problems related to lures:

Spinnerbaits. Truly a lure for all seasons, the safety-pin spinnerbait is quite popular among modern bassmen, second only to the soft plastic lures. In fact, some anglers are finding that spinnerbaits rigged with soft plastic attachments make a deadly combination. The trouble is that there must be a thousand different models of spinnerbaits, and most of them don't run straight in the water at all rates of retrieve. I must have tested a hundred spinnerbaits of slightly different designs, and only about one out of ten run true at all speeds. A few, however, will run upright at slow speeds as well as when buzzed across the surface. Why some run true and some don't is a mystery to me. It is not entirely a question of design and manufacture. If you buy two spinnerbaits of the same size and brand, and which look alike in every way, one might run true and the other might not.

Sometimes a spinnerbait that runs askew at certain speeds can be corrected by bending the wire spinner arm this way or that, by making the arm shorter, or by putting on a spinner blade of different size or design, or even by changing swivels. Another trick that sometimes works is to put on a heavy trailer, which tends to stabilize the spinnerbait. A particular spinnerbait, for example, might run true with a 6-inch pork eel trailer but not with a thin 4-inch pork strip.

In spite of design and production problems, the spinnerbait has been touted as one of the most versatile bass lures of all time, and I think the claim is justified. Many anglers make the basic spinnerbait even more versatile by adding various shapes and colors of pork or soft plastic trailers, with or without the conventional rubber skirts. I suggest that the spinnerbait can be made almost infinitely more versatile simply by changing the spinner blades.

I usually prefer a single spinner to tandem spinners because it is easier to change from one blade to another. On most spinnerbaits, the blade is attached by a split ring so that changing from one blade to another is a pain in the neck and consumes time. A few spinnerbaits come rigged with a small snap, which makes it much easier to switch blades. In some cases, it is easy to attach a small snap between the split ring and spinner blade, but this may throw some baits off balance or make the blade ride too far back. Sometimes the wire arm can be bent

The highly popular spinnerbait fooled this Louisiana bass.

up after the snap has been attached, and of course the arm can be shortened simply by cutting it off and forming a new loop. The best bet is to proceed by trial and error until you get the bait working correctly with the snap installed.

Anyhow, if you do succeed in getting a spinnerbait to run true with a snap installed, you've got a valuable lure. You can put on a large blade for murky water, a small blade for clear water. You can use blades of different colors and shapes. Nickel blades. Copper blades. Hammered blades. Smooth blades. French blades. Colorado blades. Willow blades. All of which give a lure a different appearance or action. Spinner blades themselves will be discussed in more detail later in this chapter.

Although I've caught a lot of bass with front (in-line) spinners such as the Hawaiian Wiggler and the Mepps, I am now convinced that the safety-pin design is better, except on such specialized lures as the Weed Wing. (Maybe I should point out here that Fred Arbogast is offering a Hawaiian Wiggler spinnerbait, and Sheldon's is offering a Mepps spinnerbait.) What makes the spinnerbait or safety-pin design better is not entirely clear to me, and my thoughts on the matter are certainly not conclusive, but I think it has to do with sonic considerations instead of the flashiness that is usually associated with spinner blades. Indeed, the flash effect is probably more effective on the in-line spinners than on the safety-pin designs simply because it occurs closer to the body of the lure. The sonic effect of the spinner blade itself is probably the same on both designs. The big difference is in the vibration and resulting sonic effect that the offset spinner transmits to the spinnerbait body and trailer. As I see it, the offset spinner blade transmits vibrations to the lure body and trailer by using the wire spinner arm as a lever. But that is an oversimplification. A good deal depends, I think, on the stiffness of the wire arm.

The next time you go fishing, try an experiment. First tie on a spinnerbait with a very stiff arm and attach a 6-inch pork eel to the hook. Watch the action of the eel, and also look closely at the spinner arm. If the spinner arm is stiff, it will look stiff in the water and won't be vibrating up and down. Now tie on a spinnerbait with a more flexible arm and attach the same pork eel to the hook. Watch the action of the eel and, again, look closely at the spinner arm. If the arm is flexible enough it will appear to be rather out of focus because it will be moving about a quarter of an inch off center, and this "up and down" motion (which is really circular) will be transmitted to the lure body and the pork eel. At least that's the way I see it. Of course, a good deal depends on the size of a spinner blade in relation to the stiffness of the arm, and a good deal also depends on the length of the arm.

Just now, I got up from the typewriter (my office is in my boat house) and tied a spinnerbait with a short, stiff arm onto the line of my baitcasting rig. After attaching a 6-inch, rather hard plastic worm, I cast it out and retrieved it at a moderate speed. The worm stuck out behind the bait. Although it might have had a tight little wiggle, it appeared to be as stiff as a stick. The same worm on a spinnerbait with a long, flexible arm had more action. I'm not saying here that spinner-baits with stiff arms won't catch bass. They will. But I do think that arms made of stiff wire are usually more effective if they are used with trailers having a built-in wiggle (such as the Mister Twister curlytail soft plastic lures) than with ordinary pork or worm trailers.

After I had written this chapter, I received a letter from Mr. Don Butler, who makes the Okiebug spinnerbait. He pointed out that the arms on some spinnerbaits are too stiff, and he said that some manufacturers use the same wire for different weights of spinnerbaits. He didn't go into detail on his reasons for having the right weight wire, but he did suggest the following rules of thumb: ¼-ounce heads should have wire 0.030 inch in diameter; ⅜-ounce heads, 0.035 inch; ½-ounce heads, 0.040 inch. I'm certain, however, that he would agree that spinnerbait design is not yet an exact science, and that a good deal depends on the type of wire used, the size of the spinner blade, the length of the spinner arm, and so on.

As I said earlier, I'm not 100 percent certain about the effect of spinner arm stiffness. In other words, I'm not entirely convinced that limber arms will result in more strikes. But I am certain about two things. First, a limber arm will give the angler a better "feel" for his lure. Second, a limber arm increases the chances of hooking a lunker bass if it should get the whole bait into its mouth, which can happen in weeds and heavy cover.

In any case, the spinnerbait is a great lure and should be in every bassman's tackle box. It can be buzzed across the surface, bumped along the bottom, or fished at any depth in between. If you take full advantage of the interchangeability of skirts, trailers, and spinner blades, you'll have a lure with many possibilities.

Leadhead jigs and doglegged spinners. Homer Circle once said that if he had to do all his fishing with one lure, it would be a jig, simply because they are so versatile. They can be yo-yoed in deep water. They can be fished as a fall bait. They can be bumped and hopped along the bottom, jerked along at various depths, or reeled in with a steady retrieve.

Traditionally, leadhead jigs, molded onto the hook, have been dressed with deer hair, maribou, strands of soft nylon, or similar material. All of these will catch bass, but the jib is usually more effective if a pork eel or plastic worm is attached. A jig head and "bait tail" or "grub" soft plastic attachment has been very productive in salt water for the past few years, and they are just as good for freshwater bass. The bait tail attachment usually looks something like a short, fat worm, or grub, but many are molded to resemble shrimp or other creatures.

Although the bait tail and other jigs are quite productive, they are even better, and more versatile, if they are used in conjunction with a detachable jig spinner. In many ways this rig looks like a spinnerbait, but there are some big differences:

1. The spinner arm can be removed, so that the lure becomes an ordinary leadhead jig and can be fished accordingly. I prefer, for example, to use the jig without the spinner arm attachment for hopping a pork eel along the bottom.

2. Because the spinner arm is not fixed to the lure, the jig body rides straight in the water instead of at an angle. This becomes important when you are fishing soft plastic grublike attachments, but it doesn't seem to matter when you are using rubber skirts or pork eels.

3. The hinged spinner arm can readily fold down in case a bass gets the whole rig into its mouth, whereas I'm certain that the fixed spinner arm on spinnerbaits has caused anglers to miss some good bass—especially large bass capable of engulfing the whole works.

4. The spinner blade turns while the rig is free-falling. On most spinnerbaits, the blade will flop about but won't always spin properly while the lure is going down. The blade on the jig spinner will usually turn freely if the line is kept tight, unless the spinner blade is too large for the weight of the jig. Having the spinner turn while the lure is sinking is very important in some types of fishing because bass often hit a lure when it is free-falling.

5. Because the spinner arm folds down, the rig readily fits into the trays of an ordinary tackle box, whereas spinnerbaits are difficult to store unless one has a special box with vertical hangers.

6. Because the jig spinner is detachable, it is quite easy to change it or the jig head. Jig spinners with blades of various sizes and shapes and

colors can be purchased in some tackle shops and from such firms as Hildebrandt's, Netcraft, Finnysports, and others that deal in spinners or lure-making gear. Jig spinners can also be made at home from wire or from large diaper pins.

A number of preassembled jig spinner lures are on the market, such as Bass Buster's Beetle Spin, Gapen's Hairy Worm Plus, and Lindy's Fuzz-E-Grub Spin, all of which are great bass catchers. But I prefer to rig my own. First, I choose a jig head that is rather pointed and won't hang up as readily as a rounded head. Then I attach a jig spinner of suitable size and put on a pork or plastic attachment. The possible combinations of jig spinners, jig dressings, and attachments are almost infinite, and I advise the angler who likes to tinker with lures to try various combinations until he finds one that suits his fancy and interests bass. I was experimenting in this way when I hit upon my favorite rig, which I believe to be one of the greatest bass catchers ever devised.

First, I took a Mann's Sting Ray Grub jig and removed the grub. Then I put a Boone's Split Tail Tout on the jig head. (The Tout is quite popular among saltwater fishermen in Florida, but it isn't widely used in fresh water. If you want to duplicate my rig, be sure to get a Split Tail Tout; there are several other Touts, all of which will catch bass but which don't have quite the same "thing" when used with the jig spinner.) Next, I attached a jig spinner with a No. 2 Indiana blade. Since then I've started using a No. 4 French blade at times.

Of course, any suitable grub or even a short piece of plastic worm would work, but I think the secret of my success with my rig is in the Split Tail Tout. Inspection shows that these grublike attachments are *not* first molded in one piece and later split. Instead, they are molded so that there are two tails about ⅛-inch apart. I believe that this gap, together with the vibration from the spinner arm, creates some sort of sonic effect that cannot be duplicated by using a grub with a split tail. I don't guarantee that this rig will catch bass for everybody under all conditions, but I do say that it is the greatest bass lure I've ever thrown into the water. On the other hand, my confidence in the lure probably accounts for some of my success with it.

Plugs. Most of the plugs being mass-produced these days are made of hard plastic simply because it lends itself better than wood does to modern manufacturing techniques. Some of the plastic plugs are of good quality, and some aren't. I've had bass crack them, and some have shells almost as thin as eggs. When I was doing some research

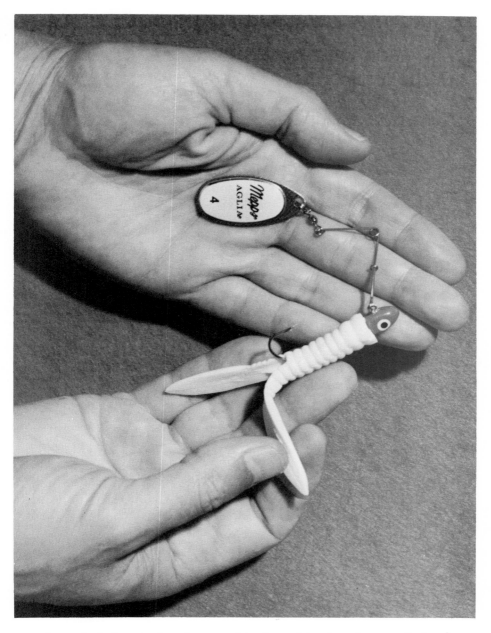

The author's favorite bass lure consists of a safety-pin spinner, a jig head, and a Split Tail Tout

not long ago, I wrote a lure manufacturer for their catalog. Instead of sending me the catalog or any sort of information, they sent me a sample lure—a crazy-looking thing with a body of thin plastic. It was crushed in the mail. I thanked them by return mail, stating that the lure was broken in the mail and that I was really more interested in information about all their products. They sent me another lure (but no catalog), and it was also broken when it arrived. I forgot the whole thing until their advertising agency sent me still another lure (but again no catalog). This lure arrived safely. It will no doubt catch bass, but I'm not going to fish with it. Why risk hooking a lunker bass on a lure that you don't think will hold together?

Some of the hardwood plugs cast nicely and have very good action, but top-quality plastic plugs last longer. The problem with hardwood plugs is that they tend to rot where the hook eyelet screws in, so that in time the hook is likely to pull out under pressure. Plastic holds the hook screws better over the long run, and, in fact, screws are eliminated on many plastic plugs by using a wire embedded in the body of the plug. Usually, a single wire is bent so that it forms the plug eyelet as well as drop loops for holding the hooks. Such a design makes it very difficult to pull a hook off the plug. Of course, the same design could be used with wooden plugs, but the truth is that hardwood plugs have just about disappeared from the market. Even some famous wooden plugs like the Zara Spook are now made from plastic. In fact, Shakespeare and Gladding-South Bend are the only firms I know about that still make a lot of plugs from hardwood.

It is very significant, however, that two of the greatest bass plugs of modern times were both originally made of balsa: the Rapala and the Big-O pregnant shad lures.

The Rapala became nothing short of a craze in the early 1960s, following an article about them in *Life* magazine. Designed and made in Finland by the late Lauri Rapala, the lures were, and are, great fish catchers; I think they are especially effective for large bass because they closely resemble golden shiners. My only criticism of the Rapala is that it is difficult to cast accurately because it is so light for its size.

As soon as the Rapala became hot, several firms rushed into production with plastic imitations. All the plastic models will catch bass, and most of them cast better than balsa Rapalas, but they just don't have quite the same action. I might add that some models of the Rapala are now made from hardwood, and in my opinion they aren't the same either. When using a steady retrieve, either the wood Rapalas or the plastic imitations may be just as good as the balsa Rapala, but the balsa seems to be a good deal better for surface twitching.

The original Big-O was a handmade balsa lure carved by Fred Young of Oak Ridge, Tennessee. It became famous overnight because it caught a lot of bass during a tournament. Cordell Tackle bought the Big-O name and produced a plastic model with a rattler chamber. Then a dozen other firms rushed into production with imitations. All of these will catch bass, but I personally don't believe they are as good, or at least not the same, as the balsa models. A lot of other anglers share my opinion. My nephew made a balsa model for me, and it has been one of the most productive lures in my tackle box. In fact, bass and chain pickerel have chewed on it so much that it becomes water-logged if I fish with it for very long at a time.

I don't really know why the balsa lures are more effective than the plastic. It may be a matter of confidence, but I feel that something had to inspire the confidence to begin with. I think the balsa has a different wiggle, or wiggles with a different frequency, when it is retrieved; and it has a different sort of buoyant bounciness when it is twitched and bobbed along the surface. Also, it hits the water more gently at the end of the cast.

Although a few local craftsmen make balsa Big-O plugs, Bagley's Balsa B is the only one that is widely available through retail outlets. Because the Balsa B requires a lot of hand work, it is the most expensive mass-produced plug on the market. Most tackle shops sell it at $5.00. Even so, Bagley projected a sale of a cool million during the first year of production! The Balsa B is a very good plug, but whether it is quite as good as the original Big-O may be open to question. The first handmade Big-Os were so fragile that bassmen carried them to tournaments in egg cartons. My question is whether a large, reputable bait manufacturer would want to put such a fragile plug on the market; if he did, he would tend to put on too many coats of balsa filler and heavy lacquer.

Anyhow, one way to get a genuine balsa Big-O is to make your own. If you don't want to start from scratch, kits are available from Bassmaster Pro Shop. It's a fun project for a rainy day.

Rattler lures. All manner of hard plastic plugs are now being manufactured with metallic balls encased in a sound chamber. The problem is that a lot of them don't rattle for one reason or another. I took a hammer to one rattler lure that wouldn't make a sound and saw that the metal balls had been left out.

I don't have any statistics, but about a year ago I checked a batch of rattlers and about 1 in 20 didn't work properly. I don't know what sort of manufacturing problems rattler lures present, but I do know that there is no excuse for a manufacturer letting a defective one get out of the plant. It takes only a couple of seconds to pick one up and shake it.

Rattler lures that don't rattle are, I think, indicative of the sort of problems anglers are going to have to face more and more frequently in the future. In many firms that manufacture lures, there is far too much emphasis on coming out as quickly as possible with blatant imitations of this hot new lure or another and not enough emphasis on a quality product. Although most companies will replace defective lures, an angler shouldn't have to go to the trouble and expense of returning a sorry lure to a store or factory.

In any case, I think that rattler lures in general are effective for bass, but I wonder whether some of them aren't too loud. I don't pretend to know how loud they *should* be, but I do think there is definitely a limit beyond which the sound will frighten a bass instead of attracting it.

In addition to hard plastic plugs that rattle, there are several bullet-shaped worm sinkers that sound off, and Creme Company has recently come out with a jig head that rattles. There are also some rattler inserts that can be stuck into soft plastic lures or attached (more or less) with good epoxy glue to spinnerbait arms or to plugs. I have also inserted these into balsa plugs with the aid of an electric drill, and they work very well. (Before drilling a balsa or some plastic plugs, however, remember that a wire harness runs through the body.) The first rattler capsule was manufactured by Little Beaver and is now widely available in tackle shops and by mail order. This capsule has a rather subtle rattle designed to imitate crayfish, which apparently communicate by making little rattlelike sounds.

Spoons. There's not much that can go wrong with spoons. Either they have a good action and catch fish or they don't. One thing to watch for, however, is whether or not a spoon twists your line on the retrieve.

Weed guards can be a source of trouble. I've got half a dozen spoons with broken wire weed guards, or with weed guards that have come loose at the soldered spot, owing to poor design or inferior manufacture, or both. Usually the weed guard breaks or comes loose when I am removing fish or when I am bending the wire up or down while sharpening the hook. By the way, the single-barb hooks on some spoons (as well as on some spinnerbaits) go through a plating and lacquering process along with the rest of the lure, which makes the point about as dull as a ball-point pen.

I would like to point out that a few firms, such as Tony Accetta & Son, manufacture spoons with replaceable weed guards and hooks. They attach by a machine screw, and replacements can be ordered as needed. That's the kind of fishing gear that I appreciate.

Soft plastic lures. The hottest bass catchers of all time, plastic worms have been sold in astounding quantities for the past 15 years. The latest design—curly-tailed Mister Twister lures—are currently being made to the tune of almost half a million a day, and a dozen or more lure companies are also manufacturing large numbers of Mister Twister imitations.

One reason that plastic worms are made by the billions is that they don't last long, so it is not unusual for the bassman to take a sackful out fishing. And if the trend toward softer and softer plastic continues, the angler will have to buy even more. If they get much softer, they'll melt in a bass's mouth, about like strips of Jell-O.

In my opinion, the main advantage in supersoft worms is that they work better with the Texas rig, in which the worm is impaled on the hook so that the point has to be jerked through the plastic before it can stick a bass. In other words, the worm had better be supersoft if the angler wants to set the hook. Although most expert bassmen use the Texas rig and soft worms these days, I presume to feel that they are just on another jag. I might add that a guy recently won a bass tournament with a weedless hook rig, and I expect more and more anglers to switch back to weedless hooks and harder worms. Hard worms stay on better and are therefore less expensive to use, and I for one am convinced that they will catch just as many bass as supersoft worms. The bass feeds on eels and sirens and even leeches that are rather firm as compared to some worms on the market these days. And there is a possibility that bass will spit out a Jell-O soft worm quicker than a worm with the feel of meat.

The Mister Twister design is one of the great bass catchers not because it is made of supersoft plastic but because it has a terrific wiggle even on a steady retrieve. This built-in action makes it a great choice for beginning anglers simply because they don't have to work the worm with the rod tip. Maybe I'm wrong, but I think the Mister

Soft plastic lures often produce stringers like this when properly fished on hot new impoundments.

Twisters are the first wave of a whole new family of soft plastic lures with built-in action.

I've recently studied the action of the Vibro-Tail lures made by National Expert, and they also have a built-in wiggle owing to the shape of the tail. I haven't made any hardness tests, but the plastic seems to be firmer than most twister-wisters made of regular worming material. Some other lures, such as the Bill Plummer's Bass Frog marketed by Harrison-Hoge, are unquestionably made of a plastic that is tougher than worm material. But it is soft enough, and the action is induced by the shape and design of the lure itself. Generic Systems, for example, is currently marketing the French-made Sosy Eel and Sosy Baitfish, both of which have a terrific wiggle. The Sosy Eel has a curly tail, and may be the original Mister Twister idea. It is entirely possible that plastic lures of this type—tougher than worms—will almost replace wooden and hard plastic plugs.

Spinner blades. In addition to their use on spinnerbaits and in-line spinners, blades are also used on the tiny lead tail spinner lures, as well as on such baits as the Lindy Roto-Spin and the Wilson Pony jigs. Tiny spinner blades are even used on the Hellbender and some other plugs.

There are several shapes of spinner blade, but the ones most commonly used on bass tackle are the Colorado, Indiana, French, and willowleaf. But there is a good deal of variation in blades of various manufacture, so that it is difficult, in some cases, to classify a particular blade as either a Colorado or an Indiana. The important thing to remember is that the shape determines how the blade acts. Generally, a wide blade turns slower and swings wider; a narrow blade turns faster and at a narrow angle to the axis. A wide blade starts turning at a slower speed; a narrow blade, at a faster speed. A wide blade has more resistance in the water and therefore tends to make the lure rise; a narrow blade has less resistance and allows the lure to run deeper. Thus, a Colorado blade is a good choice if you want to buzz a spinnerbait slowly along the surface, whereas a willowleaf blade is a good choice if you want to fish a spinnerbait rather fast along the bottom.

But shape isn't the only consideration. The size of the blade, the thickness of the metal, and the degree of dishing all have an effect on the resistance of the blade in the water. Also, a smooth blade has less resistance than a hammered or a fluted blade. The more resistance a blade has, the harder it is to retrieve and the more tiring it is for the angler. This can become important toward the end of a hard day's fishing. I've got one spinnerbait rigged with a No. 6 Colorado blade, and it pulls like a 3-pound bullhead!

Although I personally feel that sonic effect and vibration are more important than flash, most anglers think of spinners only in terms of color and reflection. Traditionally, spinner blades have been finished in copper, gold, brass, nickel, and chrome. A few silver-plated spinner blades are made, but, as far as I can determine, they are available in this country only on the Mepps lures. According to the Mepps people, and I agree with them, silver does have more flash. Here's a short quote from their catalog: "Due to the fact that genuine silver plating is more expensive and requires a baked on clear lacquer finish over it to keep it from tarnishing, most lure manufacturers do not use it. Most of them use nickel or chrome because it is inexpensive and easily applied. However, there is a great difference in the reflective light qualities when submerged in water. The revolving blade of a silver spinner reflects a whitish cast when drawn through the water whereas a nickel or chrome finish spinner reflects a black cast. Naturally the white cast can be seen at a much greater distance than the black one and therefore the silver lure is more effective. We suggest you try a little experimenting with chrome and silver finished lures the next time you have the opportunity. You'll readily see the difference." So, if you want more flash atop your spinnerbait or behind your tail spinner, buy a Mepps lure and take the spinner blade from it.

In addition to the metallic finishes, painted spinner blades are becoming more and more popular with bass anglers. I've seen red, yellow, white, black, and various fluorescent shades. Last spring, chartreuse was hot in some parts of the country, and I caught a couple of lunker largemouths by buzzing chartreuse spinnerbaits across the surface late in the afternoon.

In any case, I think that spinnerbait buffs should rig with quick-release snaps and stock up on a variety of spinners in different sizes, shapes, and colors. I might add that it may not be necessary to stock all colors. One can give a cast to most spinner blades by using permanent felt-tip markers! The marker ink works well enough when thoroughly dry, but I personally don't like the "alcohol" smell. On the other hand, I understand that good bourbon whiskey is a bass attractor!

Split rings. I buy several sizes of small split rings in large quantities so that I'll always have some on hand. They are used to attach spinner blades to spinnerbaits, to attach hooks to plugs and some types of spoons, and to form a link between a lure eyelet and fishing line. In the latter case, the split ring is used to give the lure more freedom of movement. As was discussed in Chapter 5, a heavy monofilament line tied directly to the eyelet can kill the action on some lures. Not long ago, my brother-in-law called me to find out where the fish were hitting here on Lake Weir. I told him that there were some large bass directly behind my house, and that I believed they would hit a 7-inch Rapala early in the morning. At some point during the conversation, I advised him to attach a small split ring to the Rapala's eyelet.

The angler who caught these three 6-pounders used a Rapala lure with a split ring in the eyelet.

The next morning, I looked out our glass door to enjoy the view of
the misty lake, and there he was, plugging away about 40 yards off my
beach. I stuck my head out and asked him if he wanted a cup of coffee.
"Haven't got time," he said, holding up a nice stringer of bass, including three 6-pounders! He swears that the split ring did the trick.

Although a split ring will give some lures more freedom of action, I'm
not entirely comfortable with them. There is a gap where the ends
terminate, and I believe that the ends of the wire can gouge a line if
a fish pulls or twists just right. Consequently, I tie my knot well away
from the gap, but, of course, the knot can still slip around. The best
bet may be to fill the gap with solder and smooth it down. Tony
Accetta & Son fill-solders the split rings on some of their spoons, and
they do a neat job. Other firms that attach split rings should also
solder them, but, of course, most don't. Solder, I might add, makes
split rings stronger so that the smaller sizes can be used safely.

Split rings are often used to attach hooks to a lure, especially on
plastic and balsa plugs that have hook eyelets formed by a wire harness
running through the body. Hooks on screw eyelet plugs can be replaced
by using split rings, but they can throw the plug off balance and can
make it possible for the tail hook to tangle with a belly hook. Because
many such lures simply were not designed to use split rings, I usually
prefer to use open-eye hooks as replacements. On the other hand, split
rings can help produce a "rattle" effect on lures that don't have a
built-in sound chamber. A stick plug with a hard plastic body, for
example, will be noisy if it has a lot of loose hardware hanging about
on it.

In my experience, the process of attaching split rings is a pain in the
neck, or elsewhere. Several firms market special split ring pliers, but the
ones I have seen simply do not work too well with small rings. I usually
spread small rings with a knife blade and finagle around until I get the
things on. Sometimes small needlenose pliers will help.

Snaps. A lot of anglers, and some very good ones, use swivel snaps
on the end of their lines. Although snaps do make it very easy to change
lures, I personally don't like them and can't recommend them. For one
thing, it makes it too easy to change lures without bothering to cut off
a few inches of line; indeed, many anglers who use snaps will fish all
day without removing any line, unless it breaks on them. Second, snaps
and swivels make for too much hardware ahead of the lure. Third, large
fish can sometimes straighten out small snaps. I know.

It's true that a snap will give a lure more freedom of movement, but

I prefer a small split ring for this purpose. It's also true that a snap-swivel combination will help prevent line twist, but I refuse to use a lure that will twist my line.

Swivels. Although many bass anglers do use a snap-swivel immediately ahead of their lure when casting or trolling, the main use of swivels these days is to attach blades to spinnerbaits. They cause trouble. Some of them bind so that the spinner blade doesn't turn, or doesn't turn freely enough. A drop of oil will often help a wayward swivel, but remember that the scent of certain oils is believed to repel bass. The best bet is to throw a faulty swivel away and put on a new one. It is generally conceded that ball-bearing swivels are better than barrel swivels, but I've had trouble with both types.

Hooks. Single-barb hooks are easier than trebles to sharpen, they are easier to remove from fish, and they hold a large fish better *if* they are properly set. The treble hooks on some plugs are much too flimsy for bass fishing with heavy line and stiff rods. I have had trebles mashed and twisted and straightened out too many times. Either with a single treble hook or with a set of trebles, one hook shank can be used as leverage to tear another's barb out of a bass's jaw. Another disadvantage of trebles is that they tangle too often when you are fishing in treetops and similar cover or structure, and more than one lunker bass has been lost because it tangled a gang-hooked lure onto a tree limb or root and pulled itself free. Although it is no doubt true that treble hooks will hang more bass, I firmly believe that single-barb hooks will land more big ones.

Replacing hooks on a plug is really not very difficult if one uses either split rings or open-eye hooks (made by both Mustad and Eagle Claw). The big problem is not merely in putting new hooks onto a lure, but in selecting hooks that don't throw the lure off balance or otherwise ruin its action. Getting replacement hooks in the same size as the originals is not always the answer, simply because some hooks are not only heavier than others of the same size but also have different designs. Trial and error is really the only way to proceed.

Replacing trebles with single-barb hooks gives a plug a funny look, but they will catch bass if the plug's action is not killed. My personal choice in a single-barb replacement hook is the Mustad Salmon. It has a very short shank and a long, tapered barb for easy penetration.

If there is one absolute thing that I have learned about bass fishing, it is that having a sharp hook can make the difference between landing a trophy bass and merely getting a strike. Hooks can definitely become dull from use, or from clanking around in a tackle box, but the big problem, and one that far too many anglers overlook, is that most hooks are too dull to begin with. A new hook should always be tested for sharpness. This is especially true of single-barb hooks on new spoons, jigs, spinnerbaits, and similar lures. And look at the barb as well as at the point. More than once I've seen barbs completely clogged with paint. The barb should also be sharp. Honing or filing the rounded, outside edge of the barb will help, but it's best to work on the flat, inside surface with a thin file.

There are several ways to sharpen the point of a hook, but unfortunately no single method works equally well for all hooks. A good deal depends on size and design. For the same reason, no single sharpening tool works equally well on all hooks.

I usually use a small whetstone for sharpening single-barb hooks. (Special hook hones with slots or grooves in them do a pretty good job, but I really prefer an ordinary flat whetstone.) I hold the hook at an angle of about 15 degrees and pull the point *into* the surface of the stone. After a few strokes on either side, I touch up the point from the underside and test it for sharpness. Ideally, one should have a fine grit stone and a medium-coarse stone, but either one will do. The real secret in getting a sharp point in a minimum number of strokes is to keep the hook at a constant angle and to apply considerable pressure to the point during the sharpening process.

Treble hooks are another matter. Besides having more points to keep sharp, they are harder to get at. The smaller the treble hook, the more difficult it is to get at all sides of the points. Anyhow, I prefer to use a small, flat file on treble hooks, and I always stroke in the direction of the point. Avoid that back-and-forth rasping motion, unless you are using a double-cut file. If small treble hooks are rusty, they should be replaced instead of sharpened because they may be weak as well as dull.

When testing a hook's point for sharpness, I simply prick my finger a bit. The larger the hook, the sharper it should be. A large hook is not only bigger around but also has a longer point and a wider barb, all of which make it difficult to get complete penetration. Light, small hooks penetrate more easily and therefore don't have to be needle-sharp, but, of course, large hooks with hefty barbs are stronger and hold better once they dig in.

How much I work on a hook of any given size depends on how it will be fished and on what sort of tackle. A hook that is only moderately

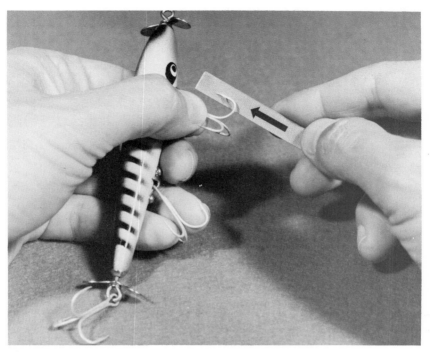

The author uses a small file to sharpen treble hooks. Keeping hooks needle-sharp will improve your catch.

sharp might be all right on a spinnerbait that is to be gurgled fast across the surface of the water; if a bass hits it, the line will already be tight and the speed of the lure may be enough to set the hook. But the same hook on a surface popping lure might be far too dull; such a lure will often be dead in the water when a fish hits, and there may be some slack in the line.

And don't forget to consider the stretch in your line. Anyone who is using a low-test, stretchy monofilament had better have his hook needle-sharp, especially if a lot of line is out. This is especially true when fishing with plastic worms impaled on the hook's point. The length and stiffness of the rod should also be considered when you are sharpening your hooks. It is, of course, easier to set a hook with a long rod because its tip has a wide sweep, and it is certainly easier to set a hook with a stiff rod than with a limber one. Anyhow, giving some thought to these matters and sharpening your hooks accordingly will help you connect on a larger percentage of your strikes.

Part Two
Fish-Finding Aids

7

Depth Finders

YEARS AGO, when I first became aware of the importance of water depth in bass fishing, I ordered a little pluglike gadget that would, according to the advertisement, measure both water depth and the correlated temperature. Essentially, it was a glass cylinder with a thermometer and depth scale inside it. The cylinder had an eyelet on one end (sealed) and a spring-loaded valve in the other end.

Shortly after the gadget arrived, I drove a couple of hundred miles, in the snow, to test the gadget with one of my favorite fishing partners. On the way, I stopped by Lake Lewis Smith in north Alabama and made a few casts from the bank. After catching a nice bass on a plastic worm, I drove on into Mississippi. My buddy and I were on a lake, actually a small man-made impoundment, early the next morning. It was cold. I don't know about my partner, but I had visions of filling the boat with bass, owing in part to the new gadget and in part to the fact that I had actually caught a bass in such weather from Smith.

But I was disappointed. We didn't catch a bass worth pulling in. In fact, we didn't do much *fishing*. All day we moved about the lake sounding the bottom, looking for a hot spot. It very soon became apparent that the depth finder didn't work properly, and the temperature readings were questionable. Toward sunset I threw the gadget into what I hope was the deepest hole in the lake.

A few of those plug things are still being marketed today, and some of them may work fairly well. But they are slow. I guess they are better than nothing, but I firmly believe that any serious bass fisherman would benefit greatly by having a good electronic depth finder. It will save him a lot of time, and will permit him to learn a lake quickly so that he can get on with his fishing. But they are not any guarantee of a full stringer or a lunker bass, and many starry-eyed newcomers to the sport of bass fishing are likely to be disappointed with them. Although depth finders are almost indispensable tools for expert bass

Man-made impoundments, such as this one on French Broad River in Tennessee, contain a lot of submerged structure. Depth finders are almost necessary to fish such impoundments effectively.

anglers, especially for fishing on large impoundments, they will not overnight turn a sorry fisherman into a good one.

The first mistake that many people make is in thinking that the depth finder will find bass. It will—but not often. The real purpose of the depth finder, at least in bass fishing, is to help the angler get a better picture of the bottom of the lake or impoundment: how deep the water is, what's on bottom, where the drop-offs and creek beds are, and so on. Instead of "finding bass," as many advertisements claim, the depth finder helps the angler locate likely bass habitat. He uses it to locate structure and substructure. Then he determines with rod, reel, and lure whether or not bass are actually there at that time.

Until recently I had thought that depth finders, or sonar, were developed during World War II, when they were used to detect and track submarines. But apparently they were invented much earlier. According to the *Encyclopaedia Britannica,* one of the first workable "echo sounders" was made as early as 1919 at the U.S. Naval Experiment Station. By 1927, the Submarine Signal Company was making depth finders under the trade name Fathometer. Although design improvements, or refinements, have been made, the basic principle remains the same.

The big breakthrough, as far as practical depth finders for bass boats are concerned, was in modern electronics. The development of solid state and transistorized circuitry permitted the manufacture of comparatively small units at low costs.

Any electronic depth finder, or echo sounder, consists of a transducer, a receiver-indicator, and a transmitter. Usually powered by 12-volt DC batteries, the transmitter produces a high-frequency alternating current, which is sent to the transducer. Mounted just under the surface of the water, the transducer converts the electrical energy into high-frequency sound waves (up to 200,000 cycles per second), which cannot be detected by the human ear or by fish. These sound waves travel downward through the water at 4,800 feet per second. When they hit bottom, or some object between the boat and the bottom, they are reflected back up toward the surface. The transducer then converts the echo sound waves back to electrical energy and sends it to the receiver-indicator, which in turn amplifies the electrical energy and applies it to a visual indication of depth.

Depth finders are classified, or named, according to the kind of indicator they use:

Flashers. Most of the depth finders used on bass boats are neon

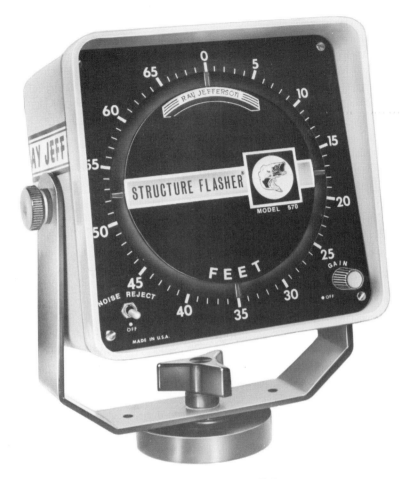

Flasher-type depth finder on a permanent gimbal mount.

flashers. A neon bulb is used because it requires only a tiny amount of electrical current to illuminate it and because it is capable of going off and on much faster than filament bulbs. One big advantage of flashers is that they can show more than one object (bottom, fish, submerged trees) simultaneously. As explained in a Lowrance booklet,

As the transducer transmits sound waves through the water, a high-intensity neon bulb whirls at constant speed behind the dial on a disc driven by an accurately governed motor. Although capable of firing 1,000 times a second, the discharges are regulated to fire 24 times per second at zero on the dial. This provides a constant surface reading. The bulb also fires 24 times per second at the point on the dial that indicates the depth, which is determined by the length of time it takes the sound waves to reach bottom and return. Although the bulb is firing 24 times per second, it appears to the human eye as an almost constant light.

In addition, echoes returned from any object in the water between the surface and bottom fire the bulb, too. Since these echoes are also timed, they show the exact depth of any fish—or any number of fish—in the water.

Another advantage of flashers is that the width and intensity of the signal vary somewhat according to the kind of bottom under the transducer. A hard, flat bottom will send back strong echoes, and the resulting flash will be sharp and bright and rather thin. A muddy bottom, by comparison, will result in weaker and wider flashes. A gravel bottom will sometimes result in wide signals similar to mud bottoms, but often the two can be distinguished because the gravel will produce a *brighter* signal. Indeed, some mud bottoms echo so poorly that the flash signal may fade out entirely. (Most of the better flasher units have a gain control that can be used to amplify the signals, or adjust them so that a mud bottom appears brighter.)

If one runs across a typical impoundment with a depth finder, he is likely to get a wide variety of flashes. With experience, the bassman can learn to tell pretty much what these signals mean. Carefully reading the instruction handbook that comes with the depth finder will help the angler learn to make heads or tails out of the various flasher signals, but only experience, thinking, and analysis will make one an expert. The only shortcut to expertise that I can think of would be to team up with a scuba diver for a few practice sessions!

Beepers-flashers. A good many depth finders, such as the Jetco Sound Scope and the model 400 Lowrance unit, have a built-in alarm device that sounds off at a predetermined depth or less. The sounder depth is fully adjustable with a calibrated knob of some sort. If, for example, the unit is set at 20 feet, it will beep at all depths from 0 to 20 feet; it will also beep when fish, such as a school of crappie, are suspended at any depth between 0 and 20 feet.

I own a beeper, but I keep the sound system shut off 95 percent of the time. Although the beeper can be used as a navigational aid, I feel that this feature is more desirable on saltwater craft than on bass boats. Although the unit will sound off if one passes over a fish or school, this is seldom a usable feature for bass anglers simply because the bass likes to stay very near bottom or in cover. Although the unit will indicate relatively shallow water, what the bass angler is usually looking for is deep water, so that the beeper is seldom of use to him in finding bass habitat. What the bass angler needs is a unit that beeps at depths *greater* than the dial setting, so that the unit would sound off when he passes over a sinkhole or creek channel.

For example, I often plug the edge of grass beds in natural lakes. With the aid of my foot-controlled electric motor, I usually keep the bass boat about 20 yards out from the edge of the grass and move parallel to it. Because I am fishing visible cover, I don't keep my eye on the flasher and would be likely to miss a deep hole. Here on Lake Weir, I've fished right over a few deep holes without even knowing it. The water around the grass beds on Weir is usually between 6 and 10 feet deep. If I had a beeper that sounded off at depths greater than the setting, I could set it at 10 feet and it would alert me when I passed over deeper water. And I've found water here 30 feet deep very near grass beds. Looking back, most of the large bass I've caught in the grass have been near one of these deep spots.

Recorders. Recorders are used primarily on charter boats and other saltwater craft, and they are generally more expensive than bass boat flashers. They are, however, coming down in price, and Lowrance, Ray Jefferson, and other firms now have recorders within about $100 of their most expensive flashers. Moreover, some of these units record as well as flash.

Although it is at times useful to map out a lake by using recorders, this feature is not as desirable in bass angling as in some other kinds of fishing. The reason is that much of the bass fishing today is on impoundments, and in most cases topographical maps based on aerial photographs made before the impoundment was filled with water give the angler a good picture of the bottom. Another problem is that the recording paper is expensive and creates storage problems. On the other hand, a bass angler can at times benefit from mapping out a "picture" of a particularly puzzling piece of structure.

In any case, modern recorders are fairly dependable and don't rely on any inking process. Acccording to a Ray Jefferson booklet,

> The graphic recorder unit consists of a sensitized roll of paper that unrolls past a stylus which changes position vertically on the paper as electric impulses are received. Current flows from the

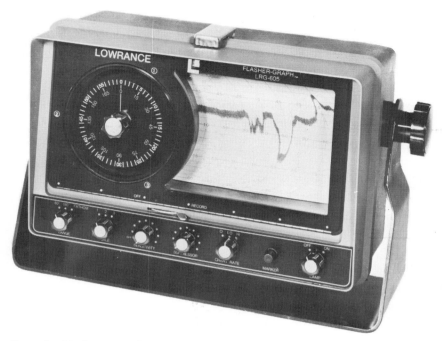

Recorder/flasher-type depth finder.

stylus through the paper and produces a black mark indicating depth. The mark is produced every time an echo is converted to an impulse. Since many echoes are received and converted in one second, many marks are produced per second. Consequently, what appears to be a solid black line is really a series of minute points.

Meter readout. These depth finders use a needle pointer and a calibrated scale to indicate depth. The needle is sensitive to electrical impulses and changes position on the scale accordingly. Vexilar markets an inexpensive Fish Scout meter unit; it seems to be accurate, but the suction-cup transducer mount is not adequate. Ray Jefferson markets two units, Models 400 and 410 Depthmeter, both of which have dual range scales and gain adjustments, and the Lowrance Model 240 Sonar Meter also has dual range and gain adjustment.

Although needle-pointer depth finders certainly do not replace flashers because they don't permit multiple signals to be received, they do have one advantage. They are easy to read and are not as susceptible to blankouts caused by glare.

Digital readout. Ray Jefferson, Southeastern Marine, Heath, and possibly other firms market direct reading digital depth finders. By eliminating the need for circular scales, these units are much more compact than flashers. Accurate and easy to read, they make handy "second" depth finders for the bassman, but they don't replace flashers because they don't show multiple signals.

A digital readout depth finder. This unit has no moving parts.

Southeastern's Model SMS 5000 is said to have no moving parts, whereas flashers must have tiny motors to whirl the neon light around at high speed. Although the digital readout units should be more trouble-free than flashers, they are somewhat higher in price.

The digital units usually read down to 200 feet, and they are said to be quite accurate. Southeastern says that their SMS 5000 is accurate to one-tenth of a foot at depths less than 10 feet!

Scanners. The latest little magic box on the bassing scene is the

Aquascan I, marketed by Stembridge Products. It is a scanning sonar system that gives the angler a 360-degree underwater view, in addition to revealing the depth immediately beneath the boat. In operation, sound waves are emitted from a rotating transducer. The echo signals are picked up and relayed, via a computerlike memory bank, to a 5½-inch C.R.T. (TV tube) display screen.

I haven't seen one of these units yet; in fact, they were not on the market at the time of this writing. In theory, however, I feel that the scanners have great potential, not so much as bass finders per se but as aids in alerting the angler to underwater structure and bottom irregularities that he might well miss with a regular depth finder. If Aquascan I fulfills its promise, then other firms will no doubt come out with similar units. But scanners will have to get cheaper before they'll be common on bass boats. The Aquascan I costs almost $1,000!

I was recently talking to an electronics sharp employed by a firm that manufacturs depth finders. When I asked him about transducer design, he stated flatly that he couldn't help me very much. They're black magic, he said. Apparently the dozen or so manufacturers of depth finders buy the transducers from a few other firms, such as Linden Laboratories. Further, he indicated that the firms that do manufacture transducers don't do much talking.

One thing that might be confusing some anglers—and it had me stumped for a while—is that some transducers are cylindrical and others are rectangular. And a few through-the-hull transducers are more or less oval in shape with a rather pointed, streamlined end. Although the shape has a bearing on how much resistance the unit has in the water, and although different shapes work better than others for the various mounting systems, the truth is that the shape, as it appears to the angler, doesn't have much to do with the electro-acoustical operation of the transducer *or* of the shape of the "cone" or "sending pattern."

The black or charcoal-colored material that the transducer seems to be made of is nothing more than a protective filler compound. Somewhere inside is a small disc, or wafer, and its shape determines the cone of the transducer. Back to the *Britannica*: Barium titanate, ammonium dihydrogen phosphate, and lead titanate zirconate are the crystal materials usually used in underwater sound transducers. To explain fully how they work would require quite an excursion into the subject of piezoelectricity, which would overly strain my knowledge of sophomore physics and would probably tell most of my readers more than they want to know about transducers. Anyhow, piezoelectricity is simply the physical principle of converting electrical energy into mechanical (accoustical) energy and vice versa. Being piezoelectric, then, barium titanate can be used in a transducer to convert, send, and receive signals.

Most depth finder manufacturers don't publish any technical information about their transducers, and the angler sure as hell can't pick one up in a tackle shop and tell anything about it. The only thing he can do is rely on the reputation of the firm that makes the depth finder. I've used several transducers supplied with various brands of depth finder, and they all performed satisfactorily. Moreover, they last indefinitely, unless they are damaged by severe knocks. It is my conclusion that most transducer problems that anglers think they have are caused by improper installation, not by interior defects in the piezoelectric unit.

Other than choosing a mechanical bracket that is capable of holding the transducer in the water at running speeds, the big problem is to place the transducer so that its bottom surface is not in contact with turbulent water (or with air). Usually, it is best to mount the transducer with its bottom surface tilted a few degrees forward; if it is tilted backward, cavitation may occur. For proper operation, the transducer's bottom surface must be in direct contact with water; air bubbles or cavitation "bubbles" will result in crazy signals, or else the unit will give no reading at all. Another problem—or requirement—is to place the transducer and cable so that electrical interference from the boat's motor does not cause erratic signals.

There are several ways to mount transducers either permanently or temporarily:

Suction cups. Several firms, including some that ought to know better, market transducer mounts that work, or are supposed to work, on the suction-cup principle. Some have only one cup and others have two. Also, some have larger cups than others—but none are adequate. First, it is awkward to mount these things on the side or transom of many boats, and the transducer is likely to be cocked left or right. Second, the suction cups don't hold when the boat is moving at high speed, or even at moderate speed, and when the bracket comes loose it puts a strain on the electrical cables and may even snatch the depth finder overboard. The best bet, if you use suction cups at all, is to tie a short piece of cord to the mount in order to prevent possible damage to the cables.

Transom mounts. One of the most popular ways of putting a transducer into the water is to use a mount that bolts permanently into the transom, as shown in the accompanying illustration. This arrangement can cause some damage if the unit hits a submerged object, and some transom mounts are designed so that the transducer will kick up if it hits anything in the water.

The exact placement of the transducer mount on the transom can be a tricky business. On the one hand, the transducer should be as far

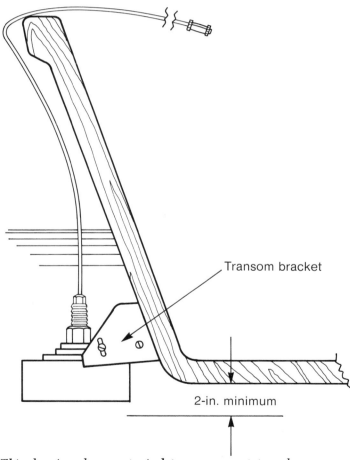

Transom bracket

2-in. minimum

This drawing shows a typical transom-mount transducer.

from the motor as possible, to help prevent electrical interference. The larger the motor, the more severe this problem. On the other hand, the transducer won't always work on the extreme left or right sides of the transom if the unit is to operate satisfactorily at high speed. Water turbulence and cavitation can completely block out transducer signals. For best results, the transducer should be well below the waterline.

I had a transom mount on an aluminum bass boat, and the depth finder just wouldn't work at high speeds. For a long time I placed the blame on the depth finder, but it was actually the transducer mounting system that was causing the problem. Although I mounted the transducer bracket exactly as the manufacturer's instructions said, the outfit just wouldn't work on that particular boat at high running speeds. After I finally put on a new mount that got the transducer down a little deeper, the unit worked fine at full throttle.

I may be wrong, but I think that a lot of bass anglers have trouble with transom mounts. In many cases the transducer might work fine if it were moved to a different position—but who wants to drill holes all over his boat's transom in a trial-and-error search for an ideal spot? On the other hand, a permanent transom mount is one of the most satisfactory mounts if it works properly at all speeds. In any case, before you drill any holes in your boat, give some thought to where the least turbulent area might be. The boat manufacturer or a good dealer might be able to help you.

Clamp-on brackets. Lowrance, Lindy, and other firms make clamp-on brackets that work satisfactorily on the transom of most boats, although I don't think I would want to leave one in the water on a bass boat going at full throttle. I have, however, used the Lindy bracket (on the transom) at reasonable running speeds, and it held satisfactorily. I haven't tested many clamp-on brackets, but I am impressed with the unit manufactured by Lindy. The transducer can be adjusted from 18 to 28 inches, and it also has an adjustable rubber bell spray deflector. It also has a safety latch that allows the transducer to kick up if it hits a submerged object; yet it does not kick up at running speeds. The Lindy unit can be folded up out of the water and secured.

Lowrance makes a clamp-on bracket that permits the transducer to be swiveled about under the water. This is a neat rig for scanning about the boat, or to adjust for 45-degree forward reading. Lowrance says the unit can be mounted on a gunwale, but this doesn't work on many bass boats and won't be ideal on any boat running at high speed.

Although a poor clamp-on bracket can be a pain in the neck, and can damage the depth finder's cables if it jerks loose, my conclusion is that sturdy, well-made clamp-on brackets are adequate for all but high-performance bass boats. They have one big advantage: they are portable. I sometimes put one on a small johnboat for temporary use, and it is a good deal better than fooling around with suction cups. Clamp-on brackets are also ideal for use on rental boats.

Hull mounts. Many saltwater boats have transducers mounted through the hull. In other words, a hole is made in the bottom of the boat, and the transducer is mounted through it. The same type of mount can be used on bass boats, but I don't advise it. A transducer sticking out of the hull of a bass boat can cause severe damage if an underwater object is hit at high speed, a danger that is greater in stump-studded impoundments than in most saltwater fishing. Some designs permit the transducer to be more or less flush with the hull, but this increases the danger of cavitation and air bubble problems.

Frankly, I don't like the idea of drilling a hole in the bottom of a bass boat, especially when there is some doubt about exactly where the unit should be located to minimize the problem of air bubbles. In short, I don't recommend through-the-hull mounts for bass boats.

Inboard mounts. Many bass anglers are mounting transducers inside the boat, either in live wells, bilges, or some water-filled space. This method will work *only* in nonmetal boats and only in spots where water can completely surround the face of the transducer. In other words, there must not be any air space or metal between the face of the transducer and the lake. Inboard mounts are certainly the safest of all transducer mounts, and they are ideal if they are located in some spot where water turbulence directly under the hull doesn't present a problem.

Electric motor brackets. More and more bass anglers are finding that they need two depth finders—one for running at high speeds and the other for fishing. Others are using two transducers, fore and aft, with one depth finder. In either case, the transducer used while fishing is often mounted to the shaft of the electric motor. It is possible to attach various transducer mounts to the electric shaft with U-bolts, but it is easier to use the clamp-on brackets marketed by Lindy and possibly other firms. These little brackets would not be satisfactory for running at high speed, at which time the electric wouldn't be in the water anyway; but they work fine at electric motor speeds, and, of course, they are taken out of the water when the electric is raised.

It is highly desirable to use a transducer on the shaft of the electric motor (or elsewhere on the bow) when fishing vertically in deep water. It allows the man in the front fishing seat to know what's under him, and allows the man in the rear seat to know what's ahead. With transom-mounted transducers, the man in the front receives a reading of the

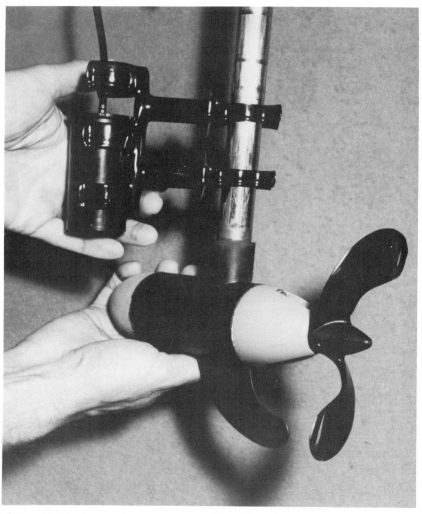

This cylindrical transducer is mounted on the shaft of an electric motor with the aid of a Lindy Mini-Bracket.

bottom, or of structure, 14 or more feet behind where he is fishing. (The distance, of course, would be the length of the boat.)

Some anglers (including myself) are now experimenting with "forward looking" transducers mounted on the electric motor shaft at an angle of about 45 degrees. In theory, a forward-looking transducer permits the angler to "see" ahead of the boat instead of directly underneath. Thus, he should be able to follow a creek bed or some such structure, fishing ahead of the boat as he goes. The trouble is that this makes interpreting the signals as seen on the flasher a whole new ball game. Obviously, the depth indication won't be accurate.

Although several gunwale-type brackets will permit the transducer to be tilted at an angle, and some permit the angler to rotate the transducer in order to "look" all around the boat, these are not ideal for bass fishing. The trick is to mount the transducer at an angle on the electric motor shaft. Then it can be rotated about with the electric's foot-control pedal. The only problem is that there is not, at the time of this writing, a mount made for this purpose. But something can usually be worked out by using the transducers made for transom mounting. The angle of most of these units can be varied by one means or another, and the units can be attached by one means or another to the motor's shaft. I mounted a Ray Jefferson transducer with a transom bracket kit and a couple of U-bolts.

Bow mount. If I had to choose one transducer mount for all my fishing, it would be a bow mount, made by Lindy and possibly other firms. It bolts to a flat surface much like a bow-mount electric motor, and the transducer swings up and down much like an electric motor. The Lindy unit allows for a variable depth (adjustable for a 10-inch leeway) and can be used on decks up to 28 inches out of the water. The advantage of the bow mount is that it is adequate for running at moderate speeds and for fishing.

As already indicated, electrical interference, or static, is often a problem with depth finders. Usually the static is made evident by erratic signals appearing on the depth finder. The boat's motor is the main cause of static, and some large motors may require electrical interference suppression kits. A good deal depends on the quality of the depth finder and its circuitry design. Many of the better units have built-in interference suppression devices, but these have their limits.

Often, proper placement of transducer, cables, and depth finder box can make a lot of difference. If you are having interference problems, try finding spots of least interference by moving about the boat with a transistor radio, which will give an audible indication of static if it is severe at any one point.

Another problem that anglers often have with flashers is that glare from the sun sometimes blocks out the signal, or makes it difficult to read. Almost all units have some sort of built-in or detachable sunshade, but most of them don't provide enough shade. Glare can often be corrected by changing the direction of the boat, but who wants to zig and zag when going from one point to another on a lake? Another trick that sometimes works is to change the attitude of the depth finder so that light hits the dial at a different angle.

One advantage of portable depth finders is that they can be moved or turned easily. Permanent mount units, however, present problems. Most of them have a gimbal mount, which permits them to be tilted up or down, but often this isn't enough. The angler sometimes needs to rotate the depth finder as well as tilt it, and swivel mounts are available. Southeastern Marine markets a heavy-duty mount that has a locking screw and can be rotated 360 degrees. The most versatile mount that I know about is the Lowrance Deck Hand made for their Fish Lo-K-Tor. This thing rotates, tilts, and turns. Because the Deck Hand has an arm, it allows the angler to change the position of the depth finder as well as the attitude.

Ideally, the dial of a depth finder should be visible from any seat in the boat, but that's a tough order to fill with permanent-mount units. A lot of boats with wheel steering have depth finders atop the console, which are easy to see when you're running the boat across the lake but which are most inconvenient when you're fishing. The angler in the front fishing seat has to swivel around every time he wants to look at the depth finder. One solution is to mount the unit on either side of the bow, so that it can be seen from either the front or rear fishing seat or from the steering console. For several years I used a depth finder mounted atop a bow anchor mount on the left side of a boat, and it worked very well. The trouble with a bow mount is that it's a rough ride for delicate electronic instruments, but I bounced mine around quite a lot without any apparent damage.

One solution to the placement problem is simply to have two depth finders, and more and more anglers are rigging with two completely independent units. It is possible to use two depth finders with one transducer simply by plugging the cable into one or the other. And a

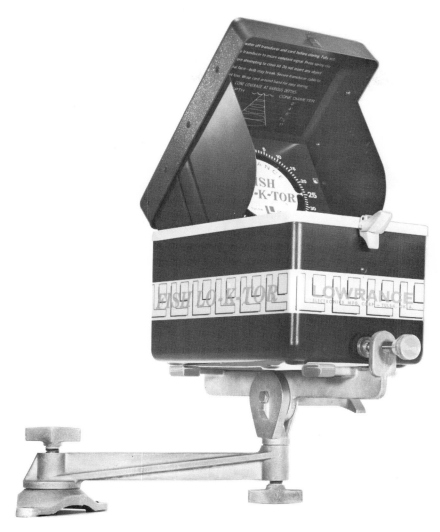

A Lowrance Deck Hand holds the famous Fish Lo-K-Tor, the first popular depth finder.

few special satellite units are available; with these, both units work simultaneously from the same transducer.

The best arrangement is to have two independent depth finders with separate transducers. Of course, one transducer is on the bow and the

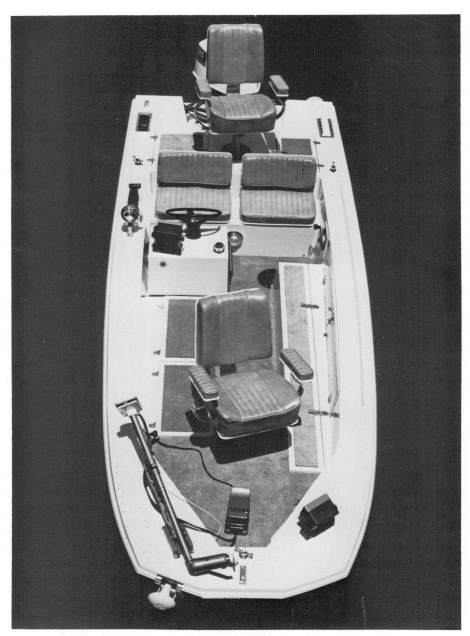

Many bass anglers are using two depth finders, one mounted on the bow and the other on the console, as shown on this boat.

other is on or near the transom. The only problem with this arrangement is that both units won't work off the same battery without severe interference and crazy signals. It would be possible to have a separate power source for each unit, but I merely connect whichever depth finder I want to use to the battery. I seldom have reason to operate both units at once.

This basic flasher-type depth finder has a satellite unit with a meter readout. Both units work from a common transducer.

Permanent, gimbal-mount depth finders operate from an external 12-volt power source, usually a marine battery or an automotive battery. Using depth finders with the power source of a 24-volt electric motor can overload the unit; anything over 15 volts may damage most depth finders.

Portable units have an internal power source. Usually, these are powered by two 6-volt lantern batteries wired in series. There are, however, a few units that operate on other batteries and at different voltages. One little meter unit, for example, is powered by an 18-volt source produced by two 9-volt transistor radio batteries. Thankfully, more and more portable depth finders are being designed to operate from either internal or external power sources; usually, these have some sort of detachable battery box. This versatility allows the bassman to use the unit from his 12-volt marine battery if he is fishing from his regular bass boat, or to rig it with the portable battery box if he wants to check out some remote pond with a canoe or light johnboat. These units are designed, however, primarily as portable units that can be used with the 12-volt boat battery. Now the Lowrance people have come out with a slightly different idea. Their 120 Locator/Sounder is designed primarily as a permanent gimbal-mount unit, but they market a battery box that holds two 6-volt lantern batteries and fits under the gimbal bracket, which makes it portable. Neat.

I haven't tested the 120 Locator/Sounder or any similar gimbal-mount portable unit, but I'm sure that I would prefer it to the portable unit rigged to operate from a 12-volt boat battery. There are, to be sure, advantages to the portable units, but they tend to bounce around all over the boat when it's running at high speeds. The gimbal units stay put, and I like that.

Many depth finder manufacturers don't publish any information about the "cone angle" in their brochures, although they may (or may not) have this information in the operator's manual provided with particular units. A few firms advertise some units as "wide angle" for use in shallow water, but they don't specify the angle. I believe that 22 degrees is about average for depth finders marketed for bass anglers, but some saltwater units have cones as narrow as 7 degrees.

Anyone with a passing knowledge of trigonometry can figure out the area of coverage at different depths if he knows the angle of the cone. For anglers who don't pack along one of those tiny calculators along with the rest of their electronic gear, here's a table based on information provided in a Heathkit operator's manual:

Diameter of Sending Pattern (feet)

Depth (feet)	18-degree Cone	30-degree Cone
30	9.5	16
60	19	32.1
90	28.5	48.2
120	37	64.3
150	47.5	80.4
180	57	96.5

8

Light, Oxygen, and Temperature Indicators

FOR PRACTICAL BASS FISHING day in and day out, the flasher-type depth finders come closer to being indispensable than any of the other electronic devices. Without a good depth finder, it is especially difficult to fish large man-made impoundments, which have lots of submerged structure. Still, there are several other electronic devices that can be helpful at times, and may even save the day:

Temperature indicators. Several firms market electronic fishing thermometers, and in their literature they talk about the preferred temperature range for the various species of fish. One firm says that the comfort zone for largemouth bass is between 68 and 74 degrees F; for smallmouth, between 65 and 70. This is, no doubt, useful information, but I think these figures and indeed the whole temperature-comfort theory should be taken with a grain of salt. I've caught too many bass in water above 85 degrees to be guided solely by temperature. It is my firm belief that other considerations—oxygen, light intensity, cover, food availability—are more important than temperature.

But temperature is important, not so much (I believe) because it bears on a bass's comfort but because it determines its metabolic rate.

When the metabolism slows down, the bass itself slows down, eats less, and is usually a little harder to catch. Generally, the lure must be dangled right under the bass's nose in cold water, whereas in warmer water bass will sometimes chase down even a fast-moving lure. Very warm water, however, will also slow a bass's metabolic rate.

Some top-notch anglers and writers *do* believe that bass are indeed more comfortable at certain temperatures and that they will seek out the ideal temperature range. Some believe that a temperature variation of only two degrees can make a big difference in where bass will be, or won't be. Bass do seem to be able to tell when the temperature is just right for spawning, and may be sensitive to temperature changes of only a few degrees. Still, I don't believe that temperature is as important as it was believed to be a few years ago.

I do think that an electronic thermometer is a worthwhile instrument for the bassman to have at hand. The more the angler knows about the water he is fishing, the better his chances of catching bass consistently, and water temperature has an influence not only on bass but also on such food as frogs, baitfish, sirens, crayfish, and the like.

Water temperature can be extremely important on some lakes during the summer months. If the lake stratifies, sudden drops in temperature at certain depths can indicate a thermocline, and below the thermocline will be a colder layer (called the hypolimnion) that is usually deficient in oxygen. Locating the hypolimnion—or determining the absence of one—was until recently probably the most important single use of the electronic fishing thermometer. Now this can be done more directly with an oxygen monitor, which will be discussed later in this chapter.

In any case, several of these fishing thermometers are available, ranging in cost from about $30 to $60. Most of them are designed to be hand-held, are powered by small internal batteries, and have a thermistor probe on the end of a weighted wire. The weight takes the thermistor probe down, and the temperature is indicated on a dial. The corresponding depth can be determined by a color-coded scale on the probe wire. Using these units does take some time, but they are generally quite accurate.

In addition to the hand-held units, Lowrance, Fishmaster Products, Ray Jefferson, and other firms market a water surface temperature indicator. This is a permanent-mount unit with the thermistor attached to the boat's hull just under the surface of the water, much like a depth finder's transducer. The units are usually powered by the 12-volt boat battery.

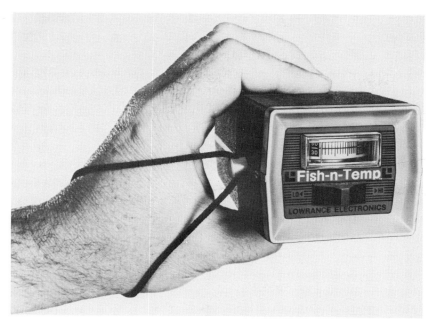

A hand-held temperature probe, designed to take subsurface readings.

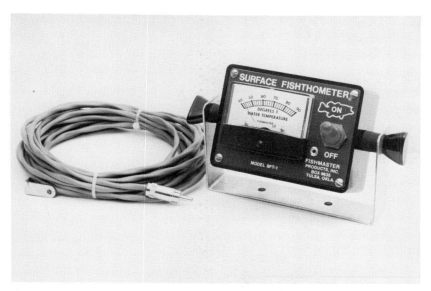

A permanent-mount temperature monitor, designed to take readings at the surface.

The surface meter helps the angler spot changes in temperature from one part of the lake to another. Such changes can be surprisingly drastic and abrupt, and these temperature variations could well indicate some condition or variable that might attract bass. Often changes in surface temperature will be caused by currents, springs, run-ins, and so on.

Although the surface units are not as versatile as probes, they are a good deal easier to use. And quicker. Since the units are permanently mounted, they are ready for instant use, and they can be operated while the boat is going at full speed. For these reasons, anglers *use* them, whereas the hand-held units are likely to remain stowed away most of the time.

Light meters. There are exceptions, as when bass are spawning in shallow water, or when they are chasing a school of frantic shad about the surface, but generally bass avoid bright light. Especially large bass. Because of low light intensity, shallow-water anglers have better luck in early morning and late afternoon (or on overcast days) when sunlight penetration is at a minimum. High light intensity tends to cause bass to go deep during the middle of the day, when sunlight penetration is at a maximum. Also, it is because of light intensity that the

These anglers are casting into a shady draw in Bear Creek Lake in northwest Alabama. Bass often stay in the shade.

shoreline plugger is more likely to score on the shady side of a stump or other cover.

Until recently, the bass angler proceeded more or less on common sense and experience, fishing shallow or deep according to the position of the sun and to the intensity of the sunlight. But now he can proceed on more exact footing if he is inclined to do so. Apparently bassman Roland Martin was one of the first anglers to approach light intensity scientifically. He rigged a water clarity meter, using a 6-volt bulb and a CdS light cell, similar to those used in photographic exposure meters. Martin made tests on 20 impoundments and lakes, concluding that bass definitely shun a high percentage of sunlight penetration.

Shortly after Martin's work, Fishmaster Products came out with their Depth-o-Lite, which measures "percent of light" at various depths. The

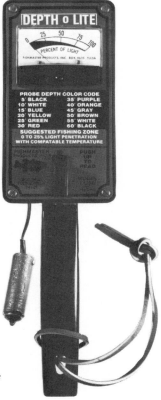

A hand-held light-intensity meter. An "electric eye" CdS cell is attached to the weighted probe wire.

device is hand-held and is powered by a 1.5-volt AA battery. The electric eye is attached, together with a weight, to the end of a cable. (Units with either 30- or 60-foot cables are available.) Since the cable is color-coded, the angler can easily get a simultaneous reading of depth and corresponding light intensity.

The Depth-o-Lite is calibrated to read from 0 to 100 percent of light penetration. According to the operator's manual provided with the unit:

> Larger fish seek an area just below the light zone, measuring zero to 25 percent of light penetration on the Depth-o-Lite meter, in a "compatible temperature" area. This is the area where the fish feel protected by darkness but light enough to see the feed fish.
>
> The depth in which light will penetrate in water is governed by different factors. Wind velocity determines the wave action on the water. A rough water surface deflects the light rays thereby decreasing the light penetration. The angle of the sun is another factor which determines how deep light will go. Water clarity plays an extremely important role in how far light can travel in water. The suspended particles in water deflect the penetrating rays. Overcast and cloudy skies also are a prime condition that determines light penetration levels. Your Depth-o-Lite will take all these variables into consideration when you drop your probe into the water and push the switch.

The Depth-o-Lite is of value not only in determining where to fish but also what color lure to use. Different colors in the light spectrum will penetrate to different depths. The exact depth that any one color will penetrate, however, will depend on water clarity, the angle of the sun, and other variables. The table below is based on gin-clear water, no wave action, and a bright sun directly overhead:

Color	Penetration (feet)
Red	15
Orange	45
Yellow	85
Green	100
Blue	180

Note that red lures would not be very visible at depths below 15 feet because red rays do not penetrate deeper than that even under ideal conditions. In murky water at midafternoon, red rays might not penetrate deeper than 3 or 4 feet. Note also that blue can be seen as deep as 180 feet, and, in fact, blue has probably become the most favored single color for plastic worms.

Anyhow, the Depth-o-Lite permits the angler to choose lures by percent of light penetration instead of by the depth he is fishing or thinks he is fishing. Here's a chart provided by Fishmaster Products:

Percentage of Light	Color of Lure
100	White or clear
75	Yellow or amber
50	Orange or red
25	Blue or purple
0	Black or dark

The reason for using black lures in dark water is that they will have a greater contrast. This is borne out by the widespread use of black lures for bass fishing at night. I might add that it is possible to catch bass on white lures in dark or very deep water simply because bass sense their prey not only by sight but also by vibrations transmitted through the water. In other words, a bass can hear a lure as well as see it, and it can home in on a moving lure without seeing it at all. But, of course, it helps if the bass *can* see the lure.

In addition to the Fishmaster Depth-o-Lite, Waller Corporation makes a couple of units to measure light intensity. One of the Waller units is combined with a temperature meter and a digital depth counter, and the other is combined with oxygen and temperature indicators. Sears markets similar units, but they look Waller-made to me.

I have used a light meter, and I learned a lot by comparing the readings at various depths, and by taking readings in lily pads and grass beds, under boat docks, and in the shady side of a stream. I'm glad that I experimented with the unit, but, to be honest, I seldom use it when I'm out fishing. I believe, however, that any bass angler will benefit by having one at hand and experimenting with it from time to time.

Oxygen monitors. All living things require oxygen, and bass make use of oxygen dissolved in water. Over 30 years ago, the U.S. Bureau of Fisheries started using the "parts per million" (PPM) system of designating dissolved oxygen content. Water can contain dissolved oxygen up to 20 PPM in some conditions, or it can contain almost no dissolved oxygen. Studies have shown that almost all fish require from 5 to 13 PPM. The range from 0 to 3 PPM will not sustain bass for very long. They will survive for only a day or two within the range from 3 to 5 PPM, but they will be sluggish within a few minutes and won't feel like hitting a Zara Spook or even a soft plastic worm. Bass anglers, then, will do well to fish in water containing from 5 to 13 PPM; the higher the better—up to the 13 PPM point.

Until recently, there has been no way for anglers to measure the oxygen content of water, unless they owned, or knew where to obtain, expensive scientific instruments. The first oxygen monitor made for fishermen was developed by a young microbiologist named Dr. Martin R. Venneman. At first the device, called the Sentry oxygen monitor, was marketed by Bass-Ox, Inc., but now it is offered in the Ray Jefferson line.

The Sentry is a hand-held unit, and works by lowering a color-coded probe into the water and then reading the oxygen content (in PPM) on

The Sentry oxygen monitor, the first unit available to anglers for measuring the dissolved oxygen content of water.

a dial. Garcia markets a unit that measures temperature as well as oxygen content, and Waller makes another unit that also measures temperature and light intensity. The Sentry lists at about $130, but the other units are higher, possibly because they are more complicated.

What surprises me about this oxygen business is that the PPM can vary considerably not only at various depths but also in different parts of a lake, not only with wide seasonal changes but also from day to day, and not only because of thermal stratification but also because of wave action, microbiological activity, and decaying vegetation. According to Dr. Venneman, from 70 to 90 percent of the water in a lake or impoundment *may* be deficient in oxygen. (On the other hand, *all* the lake may contain good water of nearly the same PPM, in which case the oxygen monitor would be useless.)

Finding an area with suitable oxygen content doesn't guarantee that bass will be there, or that the angler will catch them if they are. But finding areas deficient in oxygen will guarantee that you won't waste your fishing time pulling lures through bassless water!

Here's a condensation of Dr. Venneman's method of using the oxygen monitor:

First, survey the lake. Spend 20 to 30 minutes before you begin to fish, taking random readings with the Sentry at various depths every 600 yards or so. Diagram I illustrates this step. Assume this is a lake, and you're the fisherman. Shorelines A, B, C, and D represent Oxygen Maximums which you've pinpointed in your survey. Your best bet now [step 2] is to fish each of the four Maximums in turn, spending about 15 minutes on each. Then return to each one in turn, again allowing about 15 minutes at each location, and continue to rotate from one Maximum to the next. The reason for the rotating system is simple. The Oxygen Maximum is the feeding area. The first or second time around may not be feeding time. But keep rotating—eventually you'll hit it.

Step 3 is to fish the Oxycline. During much of the year, you'll find two distinct layers of water in lakes, inland reservoirs, and coastal waters. The upper layer will contain sufficient oxygen for fish to live, while the lower layer will be oxygen-deficient.

The Oxycline can be defined as the depth at which the oxygen content drops abruptly from the comfort zone (5 to 13 PPM) to one which will not support fish life (less than 5 PPM). Surveys show that just above the Oxycline is where the big ones spend most of their time, according to Dr. Venneman. To find the Oxycline, simply lower the Sentry's probe into the water and feed

Diagram I

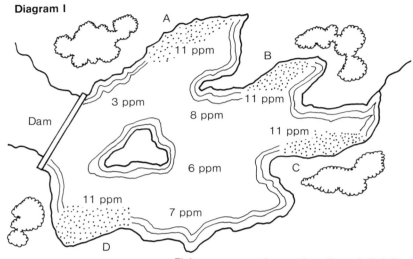

A

11 ppm

B

3 ppm

11 ppm

Dam

8 ppm

11 ppm

6 ppm

C

11 ppm

7 ppm

D

Fish oxygen-maximum shorelines A B C D

Diagram II

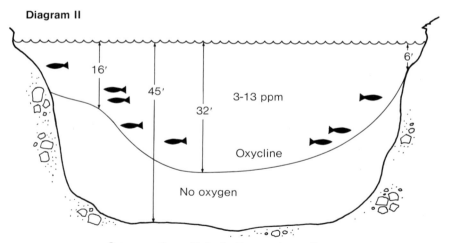

16'

45'

3-13 ppm

32'

6'

Oxycline

No oxygen

Cross section of lake bottom and oxycline

Diagram III

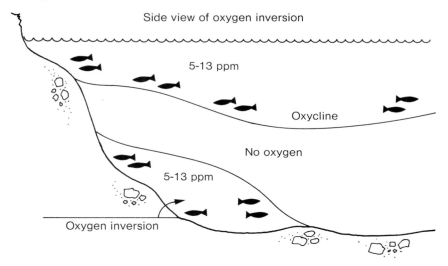

Side view of oxygen inversion

5-13 ppm

Oxycline

No oxygen

5-13 ppm

Oxygen inversion

Diagram IV

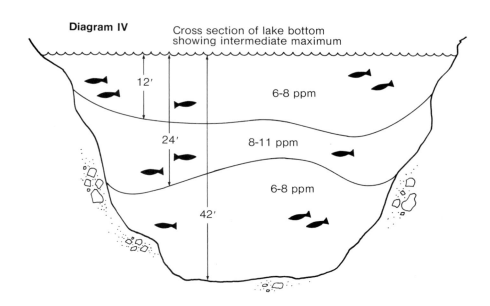

Cross section of lake bottom
showing intermediate maximum

12'

24'

42'

6-8 ppm

8-11 ppm

6-8 ppm

out the cable. As the probe descends, watch the meter face closely. When the needle drops suddenly into the 0 to 5 PPM range, stop and read the depth. This is the Oxycline. (Since the depth of the Oxycline varies at different points in a body of water, as well as from time to time, you will need to find it at each fishing spot and on each fishing trip.)

Once you've located the Oxycline, place your bait or lure just above it. If the bottom structure is good, your chances are even better. Brush, stumps, treetops, drop-offs, ridges, channels, and reefs at the Oxycline make an ideal combination almost certain to give you exciting fishing and heavy stringers! Diagram II illustrates this.

The fourth step is to locate and fish Oxygen Inversions. Occasionally, you'll find three distinct layers of water, instead of the usual two. The third, or bottom, zone is the Oxygen Inversion. It lies just under the "no oxygen" layers, and usually is rich in oxygen content. (See Diagram III.) The Oxygen Inversion is a real glory hole. Because it's formed by a rolling of the Oxycline around sharp drop-offs, underwater ditches, or underground springs, fish are usually trapped within the zone, making for easy pickings.

Dr. Venneman warns that Oxygen Inversions exist in no more than two percent of the water at any given time. Barometric pressure, underwater currents, wind duration and velocity, and oxygenation of underground springs are just a few of the ecological factors that affect them. And even when one does occur, it seldom lasts more than two or three days at the most.

The final step in the process is to fish the intermediate maximums. Occasionally, you'll find oxygen from top to bottom, with no distinct Oxycline. When this happens, you'll usually find at some point in depth a layer which shows higher oxygen content than the rest. This is called an Intermediate Maximum. (See Diagram IV.) This is important since the Intermediate Maximum is your ideal fishing depth when no Oxycline exists.

If your survey shows adequate oxygen throughout, but fails to turn up an Intermediate Maximum, you can assume that the fish are scattered. When this happens, the only thing to do is to just keep moving and keep fishing!

Just how important the oxygen monitor will become in bass fishing remains to be seen. Some of the pros put a lot of stock in them; others don't. Calibration problems and questionable accuracy have caused some criticism. For one thing, an oxygen monitor is a delicate instrument to have bouncing around in a bass boat. The probe has a 0.001-inch membrane stretched over the tip of the electrode, and this isn't exactly a piece of rawhide. Recently, however, bass pro Ricky Green, a sort of "have rod, will travel" consultant to Ray Jefferson, showed me a new probe assembly that is being used on some of the latest Sentry units. A tougher membrane has been developed, which, it is hoped, will solve the accuracy problem. Even so, remembering that oxygen monitors are delicate instruments (and treating them accordingly) will go a long way toward better service. The same thing could be said about the other electronic fishing aids.

Although I personally believe that all the electronic devices discussed in this chapter are worth having aboard a bass boat, the expert angler could get along without them, and some equipment freaks might even catch more bass by keeping a lure in the water instead of some sort of probe line. After all, a good lure is an excellent, inexpensive fish finder, and catching a bass from a certain spot is proof positive that oxygen content, light intensity, and temperature are all satisfactory. Still, knowing for sure that oxygen content and other physical variables are right will boost the angler's confidence and make him fish harder.

9

Maps and Other Fish-Finding Aids

ONE WINTRY DAY years ago, I happened to meet the Baptist preacher while I was walking across the square in my home town of Headland, Alabama. Although he wasn't an angler, he knew that I spent half my time on the local streams and ponds. He could possibly have felt that I spent a little too much time fishing, especially on Sunday. Anyhow, just to pass the time of day, he asked me when I had been fishing.

"Just got back," I said. "Caught a big one."

"Oh? Where'd you go?" he asked.

"Over at Taylor's Barber Shop," I said, grinning now.

And it was more or less true. I have done a lot of good fishing in Taylor's Barber Shop, where we used to sit around for hours discussing tackle and boats and where the bass were biting. Although I look back on those sessions with fondness, I don't do much barbershop fishing these days. But I do put in quite a few hours at my kitchen table with a big "fishing" map spread out before me. It is time well spent.

Unless you know a lake or impoundment as well as you know the floor of your house, so that you can find your way around in the dark, a good map will help you catch more and larger bass. Here's my breakdown of maps that may be helpful to the bass fisherman:

Configuration maps. These small one-sheet maps show the outline of a lake or impoundment, and often they point out access roads, boat ramps, camp sites, and so on. They are, of course, valuable in keeping the angler oriented on a large body of water, but their biggest value (at least to me) is that they can be used to help trace the outline of an impoundment on large topographic maps (to be discussed later).

Configuration maps are available from the U.S. Corps of Engineers, the Tennessee Valley Authority, and other agencies having jurisdiction over a particular lake or impoundment. Often configuration maps can be picked up free at local tackle shops, bait dealers, marinas, and so on, or they might be available through chambers of commerce at nearby towns. State game and fish commissions often have these maps available, and some are sold by commercial sources.

Hydrological maps. Sometimes called contour maps, these show the configuration of the lake and also indicate depths by contour lines. Hydrological maps of natural lakes are not made from aerial photographs, and therefore may not indicate potholes and other structure. They are, however, a good deal more useful than configuration maps.

Hydrological maps are not available for all lakes, but they are provided for many lakes by the state fish and game departments and by other agencies such as TVA. Some are available from commercial sources.

Road maps. Anglers who like to fish small streams should not put too much stock in road maps distributed by oil companies and other sources. Some of them are not accurate. For example, I was looking at a map of Florida not long ago and noticed that it showed the little Wacissa River going under a highway southeast of Tallahassee. The truth is that this river never goes under a bridge. Instead, it runs into another river some miles north of the highway. Another example: One of my favorite streams in Alabama, the Choctawhatchee River, is shown on some maps as going through the town of Blue Springs; others show it several miles to the east of Blue Springs. Both versions are only partly right. The river has an east and a west fork. Road maps seldom show both forks, and this could cause a lot of confusion among anglers not familiar with the river.

The best source that I know about for detailed road maps are the state and county engineering offices.

Commercial maps. I have located several firms that sell maps and fishing atlases of impoundments. Some of these are quite good, showing contour lines and structure as well as offering tips for bass anglers. But some are nothing more than configuration maps.

Topographic maps. By far the most detailed maps available to the bass angler are topographic maps, based on aerial photographs made before a particular impoundment was filled. Such maps show contour lines, which give the angler a picture of the lake bottom in terms of depth. He can spot underwater knolls, sunken islands, bluffs, draws, extended points, creeks, and so on. He can also locate various man-made structures, such as buildings, roadbeds, bridges, fencerows, and so on. In some cases, the angler can determine whether certain parts of an impoundment were wooded or farm land. He can spot old swamp areas (which would probably indicate a mud bottom), sand areas, and even submerged gravel beaches. Some springs are also marked, especially on maps of the western states.

But remember that topographic maps are not actual photographs, and therefore do not show everything. Remember also that a topographic map of a natural lake, and of some impoundments, might not even show contour lines simply because the depth of the water would not be apparent from aerial photographs. The same is true of some new maps of old impoundments—in which case the angler would be better off with an older map, if available. In still other cases, new maps of impoundments may not show man-made structure simply because the map makers knew that the area would be inundated. Here's a quote from a booklet published by the U.S. Geological Survey:

> According to the Survey's current map-making procedures, culture that existed prior to the creation of an artificial water body is only occasionally shown for areas subject to controlled inundation or areas that are scheduled to be submerged. Also, in some instances where a dam has been constructed after the Survey's preparation of a topographic map, underwater contours are shown in the inundated area.
>
> It may not be possible for an angler to find a current map depicting conditions prior to the creation of a man-made body of water. However, if he can find an old copy or photostat of a topographic map made prior to inundation and if he knows the

Author traces the outline of an impoundment on a U.S. Geological Survey topographic map.

exact location of the dam and water level or spillway elevation, he can determine the underwater contours and conditions that existed prior to inundation by plotting the dam on the map or photostat and tracing the elevation of the lake by reference to the contour numbers shown on the map. On completion, the angler will have traced the entire outline of the pond, lake, or reservoir. As an example, if the water level or spillway elevation is 260 feet and the contour interval of the map is 10 feet, the angler can trace over the next contour immediately uphill from the 250-foot contour. For easier reading, index contours (every fourth or fifth contour, depending on the contour interval) are accentuated by heavy lines. Starting at one end of the dam, the angler may follow the contour line until he meets the opposite end of the dam after tracing the outline of the entire lake. It might be necessary to interpolate between contour lines to trace a lake outline. For example, if the water elevation is 295 feet and the contour interval is 10 feet, it will be necessary to trace an imaginary line halfway between the 290 foot and 300 foot contour lines. Once the outline of the lake has been drawn, the map can be used to locate old landmarks that were covered by water.

After you have an outline of the body of water, it is easy to figure the depths for various parts of the lake. If, for example, the pool elevation is 250 feet, the depth of the water along the 230-foot contour line would be 250 minus 230, or 20 feet. But remember that many reservoirs, such as those used for flood control, fluctuate considerably from time to time. Even so, the contour lines show relative depths, which are often of more importance to the bass angler.

In some cases, the angler will have to trace the outline of the impoundment on topographic maps that were made before the impoundment was planned. In other words, the map won't show the dam site, and the angler won't know the pool elevation. This information can be obtained, but even so, tracing the outline can be quite tedious; topographic maps are large and difficult to work with, and often six or eight maps will be required to cover the whole impoundment. A small configuration map of the impoundment will help. It is possible that the old map (or maps) of the impoundment are being revised at the time the angler needs the outline. A list of maps under revision can be obtained, and advance prints are sometimes available.

The big problem that most anglers have is not in reading maps but in getting them in the first place. If you have difficulty in locating a good topographic map, or hydrological map, of a particular impoundment or lake, keep at it. Ask questions. Write letters. Call people. For about a year I lived near Lake Eufaula on the Alabama-Georgia border, and of course I wanted a good map of the impoundment. I wrote the U.S. Geological Survey for an index of maps for Alabama and Georgia and was very disappointed to see that no maps were available for the area I was interested in. The maps became available in 1969, and I ordered several. But I was disappointed again. The maps did not show extensive contour lines and man-made structure. After I moved to Florida, I found out that the U.S. Corps of Engineers District Office in Mobile published an excellent set of maps—54 pages, in fact—of the impoundment. I could have obtained this map booklet when I needed it if I had been persistent enough.

Here are some sources of maps and information:

Map Information Office, U.S. Geological Survey National Center, Sunrise Valley Drive, Reston, Virginia 22092. A spokesman for this office told me, "You may encourage your readers to write to us, giving us the name of the lake for which they need information, the state, and locations (also a nearby town if it is not a well-known lake). We will let them know if there is any depth information available. There is no charge for this information; we will inform them of prices of the maps in our reply." If you do write them, be sure to ask for a copy of their booklet "Topographic Maps," which gives some good information on how maps are made, what the symbols mean, and so on. They also provide, free of charge, indexes of maps available for each state, together with order blanks.

The Map Information Office can also provide: (1) the pool elevation for a particular impoundment; (2) either the location of the dam or the name of the builder (or owner), who might be able to provide the information; (3) a list of old maps that have been replaced by newer maps, together with the price of photostats; (4) a list of maps currently under revision, together with the price of advance prints; (5) a list of new maps in preparation, together with the price of advance prints.

But remember that the Map Information Office is just that; do not order maps from them.

Distribution Section, U.S. Geological Survey, 1200 South Eads Street, Arlington, Virginia 22202 *and* Federal Center, Denver, Colorado 80225. Topographic maps for areas east of the Mississippi River should be ordered from the Virginia office; west of the Mississippi, from the Colorado office. The distribution sections handle 10 million topographic maps each year, so don't expect your maps by return mail. Before ordering maps from either distribution section, you must first obtain an index of maps for the state in which you are interested *and* an order blank for maps of that state. At present, the price is 75 cents for each map.

Dealers. Many of the maps sold by the distribution sections are available from dealers in various states, but the price is usually higher. The index to maps of a particular state will list at least some of the dealers who handle topographical maps.

U.S. Corps of Engineers, Washington, D.C. 20315. This agency publishes maps of some of their projects, and can often provide information about maps published by other agencies. The main office in Washington may help, but it is quicker to get in touch with the appropriate district office, or any local office in almost any large city. The address and telephone numbers will be listed in the Yellow Pages.

I haven't dealt with all the district offices, but some of them publish data sheets on maps, and these are very helpful to anyone who is interested in obtaining maps. The sheet from the Mobile office, for example, lists all the lakes in their district for which contour maps are available, *and* they list lakes and impoundments for which they have no depth information. They also list a number of lakes or impoundments that are within their district but which belong to either the Alabama Power Company or the Georgia Power Company or the Pearl Valley Water Supply District; the data sheet gives the addresses of these agencies, which might have depth information on their impoundments. In short, the district offices of the U.S. Corps of Engineers are good sources of information about maps and map availability.

Tennessee Valley Authority, Maps and Surveys Branch, Map Information and Records Unit, 200 Haney Building, Chattanooga, Tennessee 37401. TVA publishes many types of maps, navigation charts, and related data for their reservoirs and lakes. Write for their 23-page price catalog. If you are interested in a particular lake, the price catalog will not always give you all the information you need to order maps; for example, the price catalog gives the price and size and scale of 19 detailed topographic maps of Guntersville Reservoir, but before you can determine which maps you will need you'll have to order an index of topographic maps for that particular reservoir. Anyhow, topographic maps are available for about 30 TVA lakes.

Unfortunately, no contour maps are available for the Wilson or Wheeler Reservoirs, which happen to be two of the hottest smallmouth holes in the country. A TVA spokesman told me that their navigation charts are the best maps available for Wheeler and Wilson. (In fact, navigation maps are available for virtually all TVA tributary and main stream reservoirs. Free indexes are available.) He said, "The navigation charts are used by some fishermen to assist them in locating stump beds in addition to providing navigation information. The charts show general navigational aid information, boat docks, stump beds, and several ranges of lake bottom elevation."

The same TVA spokesman gave some advice about ordering contour maps: "We would like to emphasize that the underwater contour maps comprise only a small portion of the many types of maps and related data available through this office. It would be beneficial to us and the readers of your book to suggest that they specify underwater contour maps when ordering maps for fishing purposes. With other types of maps of the areas available, we cannot make the assumption that an order for maps of a particular reservoir is an order for underwater contour maps." If you follow his advice, you will usually get fast service from TVA. Normally, orders are filled on the same day they are received, unless reproduction is required.

National Oceanic and Atmospheric Administration, National Ocean Survey, Rockville, Maryland 20852. Formerly called the Coast and Geodetic Survey, this office publishes a large number of nautical or navigation charts, and free catalogs are available. Catalog 1 covers the Atlantic and Gulf coasts; Catalog 2, the Pacific Coast; Catalog 3, Alaska; Catalog 4, the Great Lakes and adjacent waterways. Although most of the charts cover saltwater areas, some are of interest to bass fishermen. For example, they have charts for all the St. Johns River system in Florida, which includes Lake George. In addition, the charts show how to get to any number of remote small streams along the Gulf and Atlantic coasts. I might add that some of the meanest largemouth bass I've ever caught were in brackish water! Also, parts of the Great Lakes offer good smallmouth fishing, and the navigation charts should be quite helpful.

Other government agencies. The various state fish and game departments of most states publish contour maps of at least some of their larger lakes. If they can't provide the maps you want, ask whether some other agency—such as the Department of Parks, Bureau of Water Resources, Department of Public Works, etc.—has jurisdiction over the lakes in question. In some cases, you might obtain a map from an electric power company or other private organization that owns the lake or impoundment.

Canadian maps. Write to Canadian Map Distribution Office, Department of Mines and Technical Services, Ottawa, Ontario, Canada. You might also try the Canadian Government Travel Bureau, Ottawa, Ontario, Canada.

Commercial sources. Several firms either publish fishing maps, deal in them, or both. The trouble is that most of these are quite localized in their coverage, and I haven't been able to get a complete list. But here are a few:

Alexandria Drafting Company, 417 East Clifford Avenue, Alexandria, Virginia 22305. This firm publishes some 30 maps and fishing atlases, ranging in price from $5.95 down to $1.50. Some of their larger atlases are prepared especially for bass structure fishing. Their list seems to be growing steadily, but at present they cover only impoundments in Virginia and the Carolinas.

Sportsman's Map Company, Ltd., 127 East 59th Street, New York, New York 10022. This firm is a rather large map supplier. Write for a catalog.

Ole Guide Publications, P.O. Box 373, Smithville, Tennessee 37166. Ole Guide publishes a number of fishing maps of the southeastern states, and each map contains a good deal of written text. Apparently each map was prepared by local experts. Although these maps do not contain depth information in great detail, they do point out a number of features, such as shallow rocky banks, old fencerows, bluffs, gravel points, and so on. These maps retail at $1.50.

Minersguide, Route 1, Cambria, Iowa 50045. This firm markets sets of topographic maps and navigation charts for a number of impoundments and rivers; all these sets, however, are prepared by one of the government agencies listed above. Minersguide does publish several fishing maps of lakes and reservoirs in Illinois, Indiana, and Iowa. Write for a list.

Southern Guide Fishing Maps, P.O. Box 1106, Tallahassee, Florida 32303. This firm offers maps of what they consider to be the ten best lakes in Florida, and at the time of this writing they are working on maps of the ten best bass lakes in the United States.

Here are some other devices and gear that will help the angler find bass, visualize structure, or keep his bearings on a large body of water:

Buoy markers. Available from Lowrance and other firms, small buoy markers are ideal, if used in conjunction with a good depth finder, for mapping out some forms of structure and substructure, such as winding creek beds, deep holes, submerged islands, and underwater bluffs. Unless the bass angler sticks to the shoreline or visible cover, he needs at least a dozen buoy markers, and two dozen would be useful in many situations. The more markers he drops, the better his picture of the structure. It also helps to have buoy markers in two colors to mark both sides of creek beds, submerged roads, and similar structure.

The commercially made buoy markers are of two types. One is shaped like a miniature dumbbell, and the other is H-shaped. On either type, a cord is tied to the axis of the marker and wound around it. A piece of lead is tied to the other end of the cord. When the marker is dropped into the water, the lead sinks and causes the marker to rotate in the water. When the lead weight hits bottom, the marker stops turning and doesn't pay out any more line.

Two dozen good buoy markers will cost about $50, and many anglers prefer to make their own from styrofoam. If you do make your own, it is important that they work properly and don't continue to pay out line after the lead weight hits bottom. In other words, the line should hang straight down so that your picture of the structure will be as accurate as possible.

Compass and radio direction finders. Most anglers find their hotspots by visual triangulation, and then zero in with their depth finders. In very large impoundments and lakes, a good compass used in connection with a map can save the angler some running time, especially until he has a feeling for the body of water.

It is possible to use a radio direction finder to locate structure, and, if properly used, the technique is quite accurate. It is, however, a little too complicated for the average bassman to fool with. (Anyone interested in further details should dig up a copy of the March/April 1972 issue of *BASSmaster Magazine,* which contains a long, rather technical article on the subject. A back issue is available from BASSmaster Pro Shops at $1.50.)

Polarized sunglasses. In my opinion, any angler should invest in a good pair of polarized sunglasses. In addition to cutting glare and relieving eyestrain, they actually help an angler in practical fishing. I have spotted many bass following a lure to the boat, and most of these would have gone unnoticed if I hadn't had polarized glasses. Seeing a bass follow a lure in indicates two things: first, there *are* some bass in the area, and, second, something is a little wrong about the retrieve, the lure, the line—something. I also use polarized glasses when fishing lures in shallow water; often I'll see a bass take the lure before I feel the strike, so my reaction time is a little quicker.

Polarized glasses can also help an angler find structure in shallow water. According to an account in Lindy's *Catching Fish*, polarized glasses helped Al Linder win a bass tournament because with them he could spot the structure better. Here's a quote:

Sunglasses may have helped these anglers catch this stringer of bass from Currituck Sound, North Carolina.

I might insert here that after the first day of the tournament, I could have sold my $10 Polaroid glasses for a hundred dollars. I would like to add that I wouldn't have sold them *then* for a thousand dollars. (Be certain yours are wrap-arounds; they eliminate side glare.)

During this abbreviated practice period, I selected a 3- to 4-mile stretch that had quite a few flooded creek beds with underwater stumpy banks. I knew that *some* of these thousand or more stumps would have hold-over bass . . . and that if I marked them carefully using shore objects for reference, I could continue to use these bass-selected stumps throughout the 3-day tournament.

PLEASE NOTE: I said I was going to mark these stumps (they were underwater but were visible to me because of my glasses). I began fishing the last day only 5 ounces from first place. My practice of mentally marking spots caused me to win by 2 pounds, 9 ounces . . . two small bass. I was able to be the *only* contestant (of 191) to fill my limit with keepers. This limit did the trick.

Any good pair of polarized glasses will help, but there is probably not a single design to suit every angler. Al Linder said that he prefers the wrap-around kind, but these tend to fog up too often on me. I prefer the floating models with flip-up lenses, made by Foster Grant and possibly other firms.

Cameras. The water level in some impoundments fluctuates quite a bit, and during low-water periods the angler can see a lot of visible cover that will become invisible structure during high water. Photographing these objects or features—stumps, fallen trees, rocks, small draws, and so on—during low water will give the angler a record of inshore structure, which can be valuable in high-water periods. Although most of this structure will be in relatively shallow water, it will often hold bass during spring and fall, or in early morning or late afternoon during the summer. Or even in winter. (A good deal depends on the particular lake and how far north or south it is.) In my opinion, knowing the location and type of this inshore structure is especially valuable to anglers who prefer to plug a shoreline instead of fishing structure in the middle of the lake. It is also good knowledge for anglers who don't own depth finders, without which fishing effectively in open water is almost impossible.

When photographing this structure, the angler should keep written records of where each object is in relation to a known point on the bank. If possible, it is best to show some landmark in the same picture with the structure. A picture of a stump sticking out of the water, without any reference to anything else, would be meaningless unless the angler can remember exactly where it is in relation to the bank.

It's a good idea to number your photographs and note their approximate location on a good map of the impoundment. Then write notes on the back of the photograph, or draw in distances on the face of the photograph with felt-tip pens. The distances, of course, should be from the structure to the high-water mark or from the structure to some nearby landmark, or both.

Almost any camera will do for this purpose, but I think a Polaroid might be best because one can see his print and make notes on it immediately instead of later having to transcribe notes from a memo pad to enlargements.

Binoculars. Anyone who likes to catch schooling bass should take along a good pair of binoculars. Any surface action seen across the lake, or birds swooping down, should be investigated fast. There is another way to find fish with binoculars, and that is simply to spy on other anglers. I don't recommend this, but I know a fellow who learned how to fish Lake Lewis Smith in North Alabama by spying on a few of the better anglers in that area!

Part Three

Boats
for
Bass Fishing

10

Bass Boat Design and Construction

NOT LONG AGO I stopped by a boat dealer's showroom to look at a particular boat that I was interested in. The dealer didn't have one in stock, but he wanted to show me a bass boat that he had rigged to take to a local show. I knew at first glance that I wouldn't have the thing. It was too cluttered with extra seats, storage compartments, live wells, and everything he could fit in. The front fishing seat was especially hemmed in, and one couldn't, it seemed to me, swivel around without hitting his kneecaps on something.

More than once I told this pushy fellow that the boat just wasn't what I had in mind. But he wouldn't let it go at that, and he almost demanded to know what the boat I wanted had that his didn't have.

"Nothing," I said. "In fact, it's the other way around. It's what yours *does* have that I object to."

He looked at me as though I had gone out of my mind. Then he started defending all the stuff he had put on the boat. I admitted that it was all useful, but the fact remained that anyone fishing in the front seat would have to sit there as rigidly as when posing for a

155

These bass boats are shipshape and ready for a B.A.S.S. tournament.

photograph, and one would almost have to hopscotch to get from one end of the boat to the other.

The thing to remember, when you are looking at that new bass boat on the dealer's floor, is that you will be fishing from it. You'll need room, especially around the fishing seats. I think it is a good idea to get a brochure from the manufacturer just to see what is standard and what is optional. I suspect that some boat dealers are like automobile dealers. They put a bunch of options on a boat which, after they are installed, are no longer optional. Of course, some of the optional live wells and extra seats and storage compartments are very good, if you need them and have room for them. I might add that it is relatively easy for the bass angler to more or less customize his floor plan. Ranger, Skeeter, and other firms will cooperate with the angler and his dealer, often at surprisingly small additional cost.

If the angler considers auxiliary seats and so on, there are hundreds of possible floor plans for bass boats. But it can be narrowed down to four basic plans, as shown in the accompanying diagrams. There are a few exceptions, but the four basic plans cover over 95 percent of all the bass boats on the market at this time.

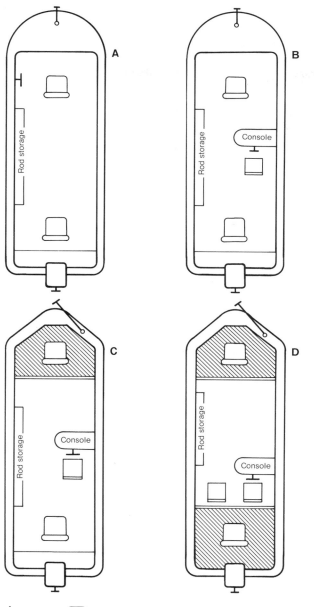

Key: ⊢ steering; ⬓ fishing seat; ☐ jump seat; ⊶ electric motor

Shading indicates elevated fishing decks.

Plan A shows the classic bass boat design. It has two pedestal fishing seats mounted fore and aft. Because the anglers sit in the fishing seats while the boat is running across the lake, the seats are mounted low instead of on an elevated fishing platform. Although boats of this type are usually comparatively small, the design is quite roomy unless the boat is cluttered with options; the fishing seats can be swiveled 360 degrees, and the angler can easily walk from one end of the boat to the other. Typically, this design is used on the smaller, comparatively narrow bass boats. Such boats are rather limited in options that they will accommodate, and they are also limited in engine horsepower because they work best with front-mounted stick steering. Some manufacturers have modified this design somewhat by moving the rear seat slightly forward and to the right, and then rigging a wheel steering console in front of the seat. This design permits the use of a larger motor all right, but if two anglers are aboard, one or the other of them will have to fish from behind the wheel.

Generally, the basic Type A design is the least expensive of all bass boats. It has only two seats, and the smaller stick-steered motor (25 horsepower or so) cuts the initial cost considerably and also makes the boat more economical to run. I believe that Type A boats are excellent choices for anglers who want a fishing boat but who don't have any particular desire to run it 70 miles an hour.

Both Type A and Type B boats have a flat bow deck to accommodate foot-controlled electric motors. In both designs, however, the seats are mounted on the floor of the boat instead of on an elevated deck. This gives these boats a relatively low profile and a relatively low center of gravity, which makes it safer for the anglers to sit in the pedestal seats while the boat is running at high speed.

Type B boats are essentially the same as Type A except that they have a wheel steering console. They are generally, but not always, a bit larger than Type A, and, of course, they are usually a bit more expensive. One advantage of B is that larger motors can be used with the wheel steering. Another advantage is that a third angler can do a bit of fishing from behind the wheel. But I've always held the opinion that two bass anglers are enough in one boat—and that the fellow in the front seat has much the best of it. (Fishing behind some of the tournament pros, it is said, is like sweeping behind a vacuum cleaner.)

Anyhow, Type B is a good choice for anglers who want a motor larger than can safely be used on Type A boats. And there are more variations on the Type B plan. I've even seen one boat, the MonArk

Target, with a steering wheel at the *front* seat and two fishing seats toward the rear!

Type C boats have an elevated fishing platform on the bow end. This puts the pedestal seat rather high, which is good for fishing in deep water but which, in *my* opinion, is questionable for fishing in shallow, clear water. I might add, however, that most of the pros use a boat of this type (or of Type D). Because this design has a fishing deck, it doesn't have a large, wide bow deck for the electric motor. The motor, of course, is mounted on the fishing deck itself, and often this design has a narrow platform space for mounting the electric rather obliquely, as indicated in illustration C. Some of these designs also have an elevated deck for the rear fishing seat, but it is not unusual to see a high seat up front and a low one in the rear. (And on a few boats, maybe with inboard-outboard engines, the rear fishing seat is on a platform and the front one is mounted on the floor of the boat.) The reason is that this is basically a three-seat design, and to elevate both fishing seats would require that one or the other angler sit too high for high-speed operation.

Type D four-seaters have elevated fishing decks fore and aft and have two jump seats mounted midships. The jump seats are much lower than the fishing seats. This is the ideal design for very fast boats, and some such seating arrangement is pretty much standard on high-performance bass boats.

One big advantage of Type D boats (and Type C, to a lesser degree) is that they usually have lots of built-in storage space, and some have live wells both fore and aft to accommodate two anglers. There are two reasons for all this storage space. First, Type D boats are usually wider than Type A or B. Second, the elevated fishing decks permit storage under the fishing decks. This design permits much more out-of-the-way storage space than is possible with Type A or B boats, so that a cluttered floor plan is not often a problem. I have, in fact, seen a few high-performance boats with an almost unbelievable amount of storage space.

A few manufacturers are now plugging Type D boats as both bass and ski boats. They are indeed a good choice for the family man who wants to use one boat for bass fishing and for pleasure boating; Type A is strictly a fishing boat. The trend toward combination bass and water sports boats is likely to continue, but I fear that too many skippers will let their kids ride in those high fishing seats while running at full throttle. Some models have removable fishing seats, and the Ranger

18-5 is designed so that the fishing seats can be moved to a lower part of the boat.

Although the basic design and floor plan of the bass boat should be of primary importance, here are some other design features and options to think about:

Fishing seats. All bass boats have fishing seats (or chairs) mounted on a pedestal. They swivel 360 degrees, and some even recline. All these seats are much more comfortable than slat or bench seats found in typical johnboats and other small craft. The back support helps, but the main feature is that the swivel seats allow the angler to face his target while casting instead of having to twist about. Also, the pedestal seats are higher, so that the angler's legs aren't stretched out or folded up. In short, the seats on a bass boat help the angler to fish in comfort for long hours. This comfort improves, and helps maintain, his casting efficiency and fishing alertness. I might add that these qualities—alertness and efficiency—often make the difference between catching a limit of bass or merely getting a few strikes.

The less expensive fishing seats are molded from tough plastic, and these are quite comfortable, if a little hard. The padded or upholstered seats are a good deal more comfortable than molded seats, but, of course, they are more expensive.

Some new bass boats are rigged with high-backed seats, in case the angler needs a headrest! The trouble with these is that they create a lot

Note the high-backed easy seats on this Glastron bass boat!

of wind resistance when the angler is running the boat at high speed or when he's trailering. Some seats are designed to fold down when not in use, and, in fact, a trend in high-performance bass boats such as the Hydra-Sports and the Stryker and the Terry American Bass Fisherman is toward fold-down seats.

Fold-down fishing seats are becoming more and more popular on fast bass boats.

The pedestals for fishing seats are usually cast from some lightweight alloy, and the designs of most of them are adequate. They should, however, have wide bases, and manufacturers should bear in mind that bass anglers don't merely sit in their seats. Some wormsters rear back to set the hook with great force, and more than one pedestal has been ripped out of the decking. A good deal depends, of course, on how strong the deck is and on whether the pedestal seat has been installed properly. Anyhow, most of the mounting problems have been worked out on the better bass boats. If you buy an economy bass boat, however, you may have problems.

Some adjustable pedestals are now available, and these are highly desirable. Although adjustable seats help the angler make small adjustments while fishing, the main advantage, as I see it, is that they permit him to lower the fishing seats while the boat is running at high speed. Adjustable pedestals are especially desirable in this respect on Type A and B boats that don't have jump seats.

The placement of seats can be a problem. I've seen some bass boats (usually economy models) that have the seats too close together for casting. Anyone fishing in the front seat can, in a careless moment, stick a plug into the angler in the aft seat. This happens often, especially on some boats that aren't designed for casting. I insist on having ample casting room between the fishing seats—maybe I'm nervous in this respect because my daughter was once hooked in the eye. The spacing problem usually arises when the manufacturer or the dealer tries to put three fishing seats on one boat. (An angler who sometimes needs three fishing seats might consider getting a boat, or rigging one, with a removable extra seat and a permanent socket, such as on the Ranger TR-3. Thus, he can take the extra fishing seat if he needs it and can leave it in the garage if he doesn't need it.)

If you have seat placement problems of one sort or another, you might consider an intermediate offset mount between the chair and the pedestal. Made by Southeastern Marine (and possibly by other firms), this mount permits the angler to move his seat in any direction on a radius of 6 inches, which allows him a foot of leeway fore and aft, right and left. Such a mount is sometimes useful in getting the angler close to the electric motor, or to set the rear seat off center when he's using a manually steered motor on small Type A boats.

Remember also that many bass boat seats are installed not at the factory but at the dealer's. And most dealers will cooperate with the angler in custom placement. So, give the matter some thought before buying.

Steering mechanisms. Many of the smaller boats (plan A) have a stick steering lever on the left gunwale and a throttle control device on the right, both within easy reach of the forward fishing seat. If the steering stick is placed so that it doesn't interfere too much with one's fishing, this is a good arrangement because it permits the angler to operate the boat's main motor and the electric fishing motor from the front fishing seat. Thus, the boat's operator doesn't have to be going from one seat to another, and he has a good view of the waters ahead. Note carefully, however, that stick steering is not safe with motors much larger than 25 horsepower. Wheel steering is much safer with motors of 40 horsepower on up, and the larger bass boats with big motors simply must have wheel steering.

With either console or stick steering, it is extremely important that the mechanism be properly installed and that all linkages be kept tight. Safety aspects of remote steering will be discussed further in Chapter 12.

Carpet. Most of the larger bass boats and many of the smaller ones are fitted with some outdoor carpeting material such as Aqua Turf, Poly-Turf, Astroturf, etc. A carpet not only makes a boat look better but also makes it considerably quieter—which is quite an asset in bass fishing. Also, some carpets are safer than wet fiberglass because they have better traction.

The only objection that I have to carpet is that the hooks on fishing plugs get tangled in the stuff. Some carpet material, however, may be better than others in this respect. Skeeter, for example, shears its carpet so that it won't snag lures as readily.

In any case—like it or not—carpet is fast becoming standard instead of optional on many bass boats, and I suspect that more and more manufacturers are using carpet to cover defects in workmanship that would not be tolerated in noncarpeted boats. I personally prefer the snap-on platform carpeting provided as optional on the Boston Whaler bass boat. My thinking is that it is easier to clean, and it simplifies replacement considerably. In any case, carpet material used on bass boats should be easy to clean and should definitely be impervious to gasoline and battery acids.

Hull. Most of the fiberglass boats designed for normal speeds have some sort of tri-hull. This design gives the hull three planing surfaces, separated by two "air-lift" tunnels. The tri-hull makes for good boat speed efficiency, quick planing, maneuverability, and stability. Also, the contour surfaces of the tri-hull give both strength and rigidity to the bottom of the boat.

Aluminum bass boats usually have ordinary flat "johnboat" hulls. The reason for this is that aluminum is not ideal for making tri-hulls because of all the contours. This is simply a matter of materials and manufacturing processes. It is my opinion, however, that the johnboat-type hull is perfectly satisfactory for normal bass fishing. The flat bottom is stable enough and fast enough, but, of course, it isn't designed for racing speeds. The big advantage of aluminum is that it is light; the big disadvantage is that it is noisy.

Aluminum bass boats are gaining in popularity. They are lighter and cheaper to operate. The boat on this page is by Fisher Marine; on the next page, by Ouachita.

Most of the larger bass boat manufacturers have worked out their hull design pretty well, and they have become more or less standardized. And a lot of the smaller manufacturers have copied established hull designs; indeed, I suspect that many of the lesser-known firms, and maybe a big one or two, have actually used another boat's hull and deck as "prototypes" when making their own molds.

There are, however, some new designs coming along from time to time. The Skeeter Eagle I, for example, has a design based on the hydrofoil principle, with two planing surfaces instead of three. Also, some of the high-performance boats have some sort of racing hull. The newer Hydra-Sports boats, for example, have a patent-pending "step-vee" hull design called Hydra-Flight. According to the firm, a stock 85-horsepower motor planed their prototype 15-foot model in less than 20 yards from a dead stop.

It is not necessary, I suppose, for anglers to know much about how fiberglass boats are made, just as it isn't necessary for drivers to know much about how automobile bodies and frames are manufactured. In any case, most boat manufacturers simply do not publish information on how their boats are constructed. And it is difficult to find out. Recently, I wrote to a large corporation for such information on their line of bass boats. They sent me a brochure—pretty but useless—and told me that my local dealer would answer my questions. Bull. Most boat dealers and their salesmen that I've talked with know virtually nothing about how bass boats are constructed. Anyhow, after considerable effort I still haven't found out from the manufacturer or the local dealer the details on how that boat is made. I don't mind cracking open a transducer or two, but I can't afford to cut bass boats in half.

I hesitate to advise anyone on selecting a bass boat on the basis of construction, but I personally wouldn't buy a boat unless the dealer or the manufacturer will tell me something about how it is made *or* unless the manufacturer has a good name in the bass boat field. I feel that most bass boats manufactured by larger firms are adequately made. On the other hand, a lot of small outfits are springing up all over the country, especially in the South and Southwest, that do not have a reputation and that don't even publish brochures. I wouldn't advise anyone to buy one of these—and certainly not the high-performance models—unless he knows something about the firm or about how the boats are made. I'm not against small firms, some of which might grow into big ones. Ranger Boats, for example, started out only a few years ago, and today it is one of the largest firms in the business. Why? Because they make good boats and know what bass anglers want or need.

I would also advise anyone to look very carefully at any bass boat made by a boat manufacturer whose reputation was made in other types of boats. I suspect that they often try to make bass boats on one of their proven hulls, so that they won't have to go to the expense of making new molds. These boats may be extremely well constructed, but their floor plan is likely to leave something to be desired. For example, an acknowledged leader in saltwater craft has introduced a "bass boat" into their line. Although the construction is great, the design is lousy for bass fishing. They haven't made good use of potential storage space, and their bow deck design just won't do. Instead of a flat, smooth surface in front of the fishing seat, their bow deck has steps in it. The steps are caused by an elevated lid for a storage compartment stuck in right where it ought not to be. It is very difficult to use a foot-controlled electric motor on this boat simply because there is no place to put the foot pedal so that it will be on a flat surface within easy reach of the fishing chair. Either this firm tried to make a bass boat in an existing mold or they didn't know anything about the requirements of bass anglers—or both. In this case, an angler who relied on the firm's reputation as a boat builder would end up with an expensive craft that would not be ideally suited to bass fishing.

If anyone wants to delve further into construction details, he might question dealers and manufacturers on the following important details:

Stringers. Because fiberglass is a flexible material, it needs a stiffener when it is used on the bottom of a bass boat. Wooden strips—usually three—are placed longitudinally and bonded to the hull. They should be completely surrounded by fiberglass to increase their strength and to protect them from moisture. These stringers are usually made from plywood, but fir and possibly other woods are also used.

If a bass boat doesn't have enough stringers, it can be too weak structurally. Although the danger of outright failure may be small, the hull can warp or buckle under a load or while sitting on a trailer. Some boats form a "bottom hook" that can destroy the hull's planing design.

Flotation. Up until recently, I thought that virtually all bass boats had foam flotation injected into the void between hull and deck. This is not always the case. Many boats have foam blocks placed in them by hand, and this may be the better method because it leaves air spaces that permit the inside of the boat to dry out if it gets wet or moist.

Injected foam might provide more buoyancy if it is put in properly.

Most modern bass boats of top quality have upright flotation.

I've read that there should be six or eight injection points so that the foam will completely fill the void.

The big problem with injected foam is that if the boat springs a leak —which isn't unheard of on fiberglass boats—the foam gradually soaks up water like a sponge. This makes a big mess, and there's no easy way to dry it out. A friend of mine ran into this problem. His new fiberglass boat sprang a small leak, and the foam soaked up water. He couldn't dry it out, and eventually it rotted a plywood decking. He tried to get some sort of settlement, but the boat manufacturer wouldn't help him and neither would the Better Business Bureau. He ended up cutting the deck out of the boat. After things had dried out, he put the boat back together with fiberglass cloth and epoxy resin.

I'm not saying that one shouldn't buy a boat with injected foam. If it stays dry and is properly injected, it is the best flotation available. But I would advise anyone to determine whether the wooden stringers (and any other wood exposed to the foam) are completely covered with fiberglass to prevent rotting. I would also advise him to find out what sort of foam is used. Boston Whaler, for example, fills their hull with a foam that won't absorb water and is not harmed by gasoline or oil.

Transom. The transom should be the strongest part of a bass boat, and especially on high-performance jobs. The larger the motor, the stronger the transom should be. Virtually all fiberglass boats have some plywood in the transom, up to thicknesses of $1\frac{1}{2}$ inches or more. Also, the plywood is usually—and certainly should be—heavily reinforced with fiberglass cloth or matting impregnated with resin.

And merely having an adequate thickness and strength to withstand the vibrational fatigue stress (if that's the term) set up by the motor isn't enough. The transom reinforcements should be adequately bonded to the sides and bottom of the boat to help prevent damage in case the motor hits a submerged object at high speed. More than one transom has been jerked out of a bass boat.

Fabrication technique. Although a few large boat companies may mass-produce boats by forming fiberglass between elaborate male and female molds, most of the bass boats are made either by laying the fiberglass into the mold and then impregnating it with resin or by spraying on a mixture of fiberglass and resin. Neither technique is exact, so that the quality of the boat will depend largely on the workmanship and the materials used. The problem with spray work is that the thickness of the hull can vary from boat to boat, and from spot to spot on a particular boat. For this reason, I lean toward the hand lay-up technique. But, as I said, a good deal depends on quality workmanship.

Regardless of fabrication technique, I prefer to have a good thick hull. I know one angler who talked a bass boat manufacturer into reducing the fiberglass and resin in one of the firm's regular high-performance boats. The object was to make the boat lighter so that it would run faster—at the expense of hull thickness and strength. The owner said the boat would run well over 70 miles per hour! I would no more get in that thing with him than I would get on a motorcycle with Evel Knievel.

11

Motors
and
Bass Boat
Accessories

IF I HAD TO FISH either from a $7,000 bass boat rigged with everything *except* a bow-mounted electric motor or with a $200 ordinary johnboat equipped with nothing but an electric, I wouldn't have to think very long. I would take the johnboat and the electric. Of course, I would prefer to fish from a full rig, but a bass boat without an electric on the bow simply isn't complete. A bow-mounted electric motor isn't merely another accessory to catch the bassman's fancy. It is necessary to the concept of the bass boat, and it goes a long way toward making the modern bass boat the world's most efficient fishing machine. A foot-controlled electric motor helps me get in twice as many effective casts during a day's fishing. The reason is simply that the foot-control unit permits me to keep both hands free for casting and retrieving a lure instead of having to keep the boat in position with a paddle or with oars.

I've never had much use for an electric motor mounted on the transom of a boat. They do beat paddling—but not very much. There is, however, a neat system of mounting a manually steered electric motor

170

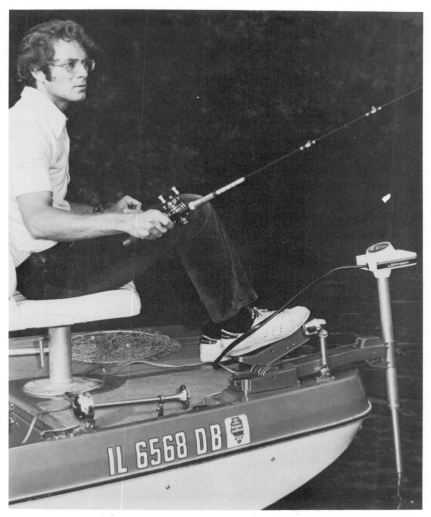

This angler is using a bow-mounted, foot-controlled electric motor. A bass boat simply isn't complete without an electric on the bow.

on the bow and rigging it with foot-controlled start-stop switches. This system will be discussed later in this chapter.

There are at least 16 firms in this country that make electric motors, and some of these offer a number of different models. Minn-Kota, for example, currently offers 11 different motors. Since such a wide choice is available, I think the angler should shop around before buying. After all, some of the better electrics sell for $250 or more, and it is unwise to pay that much money for a particular motor when another might suit your needs a little better. Or a lot better. Say, for example, that you have rigged a 10-foot johnboat for fishing in small ponds. You've put a bow bracket up front to accommodate a foot-controlled unit, and you have put your battery, depth finder, and other gear in the front or mid-sections of the boat. You want to sit in the rear so that you will be in a convenient spot from which to operate the kicker, so you have mounted your fishing seat atop the rear slat seat. You've got a great little fishing rig, but if you buy or order a foot-controlled electric motor without giving the matter some thought, you will be in for a disappointment. Most electrics don't have control cables long enough to reach from the bow back to the rear seat of your rig. If you had done your homework, however, you would have learned that Shakespeare makes a motor with an 8-foot cable, which is about what you would need. On the other hand, if you had ordered this particular motor for use on a regular bass boat, you would end up with far too much cable for front-seat operation. It would get in your way, and might trip you up.

One common mistake is to buy a motor that doesn't have a shaft long enough for your boat. I fished with one motor that worked fine in calm weather, but when the wind was up the prop sputtered around on the surface as much as it stayed submerged in the water. Unless you know *exactly* what you need, the best bet is to get a motor with a long, adjustable shaft. Even if the shaft is too long for your present boat, the depth of the prop can be adjusted—and, who knows, you may need the extra shaft when you buy a bigger bass boat.

Here are some points to consider:

Mounting devices. By far the majority of foot-controlled electrics have a permanent bow-mounting system. In my opinion, this is the most satisfactory way to put an electric on a bass boat, and most of the mounting brackets permit the angler to raise and lower the motor quickly and easily. These mounting systems, however, require a flat surface that is flush with, or maybe slightly above, the top of the bow gunwale. This rules them out for boats that do not have such a mounting surface, although some sort of elevated bracket can often be installed to accommodate a bow-mount motor. Fisher Marine, for example, sells a little metal bracket with a flat top that can be mounted on the front deck of an aluminum johnboat. The biggest problem here is mounting a foot-controlled electric on boats of the semi-vee design.

Most true bass boats are designed to accept bow-mounted electrics, and they are ideal. The only disadvantage that I can see is that a bow mount rather permanently fixes the motor to the boat. In other words, the motor can't readily be taken off and put onto another boat should the occasion arise. For this reason, some bass anglers might want to consider getting a transom-mount foot-controlled electric and using it

This jaunty angler was using a transom-mount electric on the bow. Note the piece of wood attached to the left side of the bow.

on the bow. Again, mounting can be a problem, but something can usually be worked out. Special mounting brackets are available from Southeastern Marine and other firms. I once used a piece of 2-by-4 wood on a johnboat to accommodate a transom-mount motor, and it worked very well. I could easily remove the motor for use on the forward gunwale of a rental boat, or on another angler's boat.

You may have to shop around, however, to find a transom-mount or "clamp-on" foot-controlled electric. Byrd, Minn-Kota, and possibly other firms make them, but they are difficult to find in stock at marine dealers. The Motor-Guide people marketed a neat Porta-Pak foot-controlled electric, but they have discontinued it.

Speed controls. Because the bass angler frequently starts and stops his electric merely by applying pressure on the foot pedal, he could get along quite nicely with only one speed setting—high. A few inexpensive motors are made with only one speed, but all foot-controlled units have at least two, high and low, and many have high, medium, and low. Some of the Pflueger motors have six forward speeds, and an Electra Pal model has ten!

I have recently used a new Minn-Kota 555, and it has a switch as well as a rheostat knob. The knob allows for infinite adjustment within a certain range, so that the angler can ease along a shoreline with the motor running continuously instead of having to start and stop to adjust his forward progress. The switch on this motor has two positions. One switches the control to the rheostat, and the other is a special high-speed setting for moving along at a clip. It's a neat arrangement. I like a rheostat control, but I wouldn't buy or reject a particular motor on that basis alone. Anyhow, several firms market motors with variable speed controls.

Direction indicators. All the foot-controlled electrics that I have ever used (except for a transom-mount motor with a foot-control accessory) have some sort of direction indicator. Many have mechanical pointers atop the head, and these are quite adequate for most fishing. Bass anglers who fish a lot at night, however, may prefer to have some sort of lighted direction indicator. These are available on some models of Shakespeare, Evinrude, Pflueger, and others. Some bassmen who frequently fish at night prefer a motor with manual steering but with foot-controlled start-stop switches; these will be discussed later in this chapter.

Permanent magnets. Most bass anglers start and stop their motors many times during the course of a day's fishing. The more a motor is started and stopped, the more desirable it becomes to have a permanent magnet in it, simply because no electrical energy is required from the battery to create the magnetic field. With regular field-wound motors, amperes must be drained from the battery to energize the magnet. Consequently, permanent magnet motors use from 20 to 25 percent less battery power, which can be important on all-day bass fishing trips.

Voltage. Most bass anglers own 12-volt motors, and these are normally quite satisfactory for all but large bass boats. The trend, however, is toward the larger boats and 24-volt motors. Some 24-volt motors have a toggle selector switch to convert them to operate on 12-volt batteries. In many respects, the big new motors are a good choice not only for anglers who own large boats (or expect to get one) but also for those who want extra power—maybe for trolling or for fishing in swift streams —on a smaller bass boat.

But a lot of anglers who buy 24-volt motors don't know what they are getting themselves into. First, 24-volt motors require two 12-volt batteries wired in series, and this complicates things for anglers who want to operate the main engine ignition system, depth finders, and boat lights from the same power source. A 24-volt system can severely overload circuits, blow fuses, and may even burn out the starter motor.

The two-battery system also presents problems in charging. As far as I know, a 24-volt charger is not available, so that the best bet is to disconnect all the wiring and charge each battery separately. Or you can rewire the batteries in parallel and charge both simultaneously with a 12-volt charger. In either case, charging a 2-battery system is not as convenient as charging a single 12-volt battery.

Using one of the two batteries to power the starter motor on your main engine also presents problems in using the engine's alternator to recharge the batteries while the boat is running from one fishing hole to another. It can be done, but the batteries have to be rewired in parallel. They also have to be rewired in parallel if you use your automobile to recharge the boat batteries while driving to and from the lake. (With a single battery, this can be done by running jumpers from the automobile battery back to the boat trailer.)

But all this can be worked out by a competent marine dealer or by someone who specializes in rigging bass boats. In my opinion, the best bet is to have *three* 12-volt batteries if you own a large boat. One is used for boat lights, depth finders, and engine ignition. The other two are wired in series to run the 24-volt electric—and *only* the electric. The fuse-blowing problems usually arise when you try to operate both 24- and 12-volt systems from a 2-battery pack.

I own a new 24-volt Pflueger motor, and I like the extra thrust it offers. But for normal bass fishing on a normal-size bass boat, I usually use it with only one 12-volt battery. If I need extra thrust, I wire in the extra battery and flip the toggle switch to 24-volt operation.

Amp draw and thrust. Although some electric motors and their props are more efficient than others, the amp draw usually determines the thrust of the unit. The higher the speed, the more the thrust—but the greater the amp drain on the battery.

Bass anglers who are considering a 24-volt motor might instead consider a 12-volt motor with a high amp rating. Although most 12-volt electrics draw from 10 to 20 amps at high speed, a few are a good deal more powerful. The Shakespeare Model 612, for example, draws 23 amps at high speed, generating 15 pounds of thrust, whereas their Model 52 draws only 10 amps and generates 5.5 pounds of thrust. The TrolMaster Mark XX is, as far as I know, the most powerful 12-volt electric on the market. Actually two motors mounted on one shaft and operating from a single battery, the unit draws 32 amps at high speed and generates 42 pounds of thrust!

Note, however, that the thrust figures published by one firm or another are to be taken with a grain of salt. There are as yet no established industry standards for determining thrust, and some reliable manufacturers don't publish thrust data at all. When determining the thrust of an electric, a good deal depends on the conditions under which the motor is tested; for example, an electric will produce a higher thrust when it is cold than when it is hot.

If your battery is rated at, say, 60 ampere-hours, it will run a 32 amp motor at high speed for only about 2 hours *if* it is fully charged at the outset. The same battery would operate a 10-amp motor at high speed for 6 hours. (Figure this by dividing the motor rating into the battery rating.) So, if you want to fish from sunup until sundown with a large, powerful motor, you had better get a large battery or else use two batteries wired in parallel. Batteries for use on bass boats will be discussed on pages 182–83.

Weed guard. One of the most useful accessories I own is an inexpensive electric motor weed guard, made by Weed Master. It is available for motors with the following outside diameters (in inches): 2½, 3, 3½, 4, and 4½.

Although the motor guard does cut down on boat speed somewhat, it is most useful for fishing in weed beds. It will take a boat through surprisingly thick stuff, but it's a good idea to raise the main motor out of the water so that the electric won't have too much pulling to do. The weed guard has helped me land several lunker bass out of weed beds simply because it enabled me to get back to them, which can be a real problem if you are fishing alone. The weed guard is also good protection against silt and monofilament fishing line, which can choke an electric motor up and thereby cause it to overheat. Monofilament wound around the shaft can even cut the seal, causing water to leak into the interior of the motor. This is bad news.

Although I personally am sold on a good foot-controlled electric motor, there is another rig that works better for some anglers. It is a bow-mount electric with manual steering and foot-controlled on-off switches. The system works best with two foot-operated switches, one on either side of the bow deck and within easy reach of either side of the forward fishing chair. Thus, the angler can start and stop the motor with either foot, depending on whether he is fishing to the right or left of the boat. The rig works beautifully until the angler wants to change direction. Then he must move the motor's steering handle with his hand (or possibly nudge it with his foot). But this takes only a second, and, for some types of fishing, the angler doesn't have to change directions constantly.

It's a neat, clean rig, and a lot of top-notch bassmen prefer it over a foot-controlled steering system. There are some real advantages: (1) The rig is cheaper and less complicated than a foot-controlled, or foot-steered, unit. (2) It doesn't clutter the bow of the boat. (3) It is not as tiring to use for long periods of time. (4) The two switches can be mounted in an ideal position for right- or left-foot operation, whereas there is no ideal place to mount a single foot-control pedal for use with either foot. (5) It is easier to use while one is standing up to fish—and anyone who has tried to fish with one foot on the deck and the other on a 45-degree foot pedal will admit that remote steering leaves something to be desired in this respect. (6) Manual steering gives the angler a more positive sense of direction for night fishing, although, as was pointed out earlier in this chapter, foot-controlled units with lighted direction indicators are now available.

The obvious disadvantage of the rig is that the angler does not have both hands free for fishing at all times, but this is not usually as much of a problem when he is fishing over deep-water structure as when he is hugging a shoreline. I might add here that I use a foot-control when trying to work a lunker bass out of cover or away from obstructions, and at a time like this I don't want to have to maneuver the boat with a manually steered motor. In short, I want both hands on my rod and reel.

One potential problem with a foot-switch, manually steered motor is that it can't be used successfully on some bass boat designs simply because the seat can't be mounted close enough to the bow. The motor's handle *must* be within easy reach, whereas the position of the seat isn't as critical with foot-controlled units. The rig simply will not work satisfactorily with boats that have the fishing seat mounted behind a wide bow deck. It works best on boats with the fishing seat mounted atop an elevated deck, so that the seat can be positioned close to the front of the boat. Most manufacturers (or dealers) mount the seat on such a boat a good ways back to make room for a foot pedal, so the angler may have trouble finding a fully rigged boat suitable for manual steering. The best bet is to have the seat custom mounted.

Another possibility is to buy an offset mount so that the seat can be moved up slightly, or back slightly. Such mounts were discussed in Chapter 10.

A few years ago, most bass boats used outboard motors of 20 or 25 horsepower. Today 70 is about average, and 135 is certainly not uncommon. I suggest that the angler buy a motor of the maximum horsepower recommended by the manufacturer for a particular boat. If he exceeds the maximum rating, the boat could be dangerous. If he goes too far under the maximum rating, the boat will not plane properly or operate efficiently. For the most efficient operation, a boat should have a motor large enough to plane it properly without going full throttle. But too many bass anglers run a boat motor wide open too much of the time.

For several years, I fished quite satisfactorily with a little 14-foot Fisher Marine Swift Bass Boat and a 9.8 Mercury (the firm recommended a 10-horsepower motor). The rig worked beautifully, but most bass boats are bigger and much heavier and therefore require a bigger motor. The angler who needs a small motor has a wide choice, but the choice narrows drastically with motors over 20 horsepower. Except for the Montgomery Ward 35- and 55-horsepower Sea Kings, all the bigger outboards made in this country are Mercury, Chrysler, Johnson, or

Evinrude. (The 55-horsepower Bearcat is unfortunately no longer in production.) All of the big motors are very good, and they are getting even better. For the past few years, they have increased in efficiency by 5 or 6 percent annually. They are getting lighter and more dependable, use gas-oil ratios of 50 to 1, have improved ignition systems, and are less noisy. Of course, any machine as complicated as a reciprocating

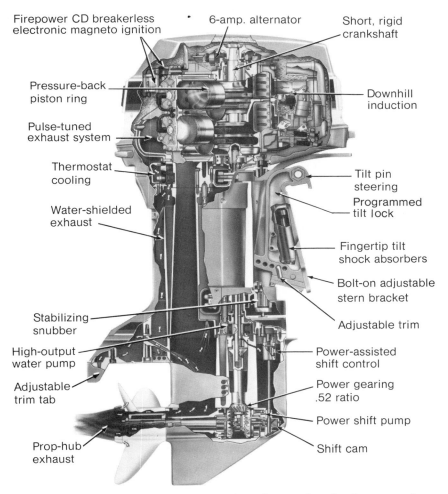

Firepower CD breakerless electronic magneto ignition

6-amp. alternator

Short, rigid crankshaft

Pressure-back piston ring

Downhill induction

Pulse-tuned exhaust system

Thermostat cooling

Tilt pin steering

Programmed tilt lock

Water-shielded exhaust

Fingertip tilt shock absorbers

Bolt-on adjustable stern bracket

Stabilizing snubber

Adjustable trim

High-output water pump

Power-assisted shift control

Adjustable trim tab

Power gearing .52 ratio

Power shift pump

Prop-hub exhaust

Shift cam

This cutaway illustration shows a typical modern outboard. This particular model is an Evinrude 135.

engine is bound to give trouble from time to time. There has been a lot of talk about Wankel-engine outboards, but so far they simply have not materialized.

The main thing is to buy a motor that is compatible with one's boat, and to keep it in good shape. There is nothing more aggravating on a fishing trip than a motor that won't crank. I think an outboard (and the inboard-outboards too) should be run at least once a week, and should have a good inspection and tune-up at least once a year. Either take it to an authorized mechanic, or obtain a maintenance manual and learn to do it yourself.

Although I won't recommend one company's motor over another, for the same reason that I wouldn't recommend a Ford over a Chevrolet, I do think that the angler should look carefully at the options and accessories that are available for modern motors:

Power trim and tilt. For maximum operating efficiency, a boat should be properly trimmed; that is, the motor should be set at the proper drive angle so that the amount of hull touching the water at a given running speed is held to a minimum. Most anglers set their motors annually for what they think is an optimum position and then forget it. However, load distribution, additional weight, boat speed, and other factors can alter the ideal drive angle. A power trim makes it easy to adjust the motor's angle, so that anglers are more likely to keep the motor at the right setting if they have power trim.

A power trim system consists of hydraulic cylinders, a pump powered by the boat's battery, and a remote control. Thus, the angler has finger-tip control of his boat's trim.

Some units have a power trim and power tilt in the same package, and some have a separate power tilt. It is, of course, nice to have a power tilt to raise the prop high for launching, trailering, beaching, or for running at slow speeds in shallow or stump-studded water. It is also valuable for getting the prop out of the water when you hook into a lunker bass on light tackle!

Power trim (and tilt) is standard on some motors, and optional on others. Kits are also available. However, power trim is generally not available for motors smaller than 50 horsepower. (Evinrude, for example, has an optional power tilt for its 40-horsepower motors, but this is a tilt only. Their 50-horsepower motors have an optional power trim and tilt combined, or a power tilt alone. All their larger motors have optional trim and tilt combined. All Mercury motors from 50 horse-power on up have power trim and tilt either as standard or as optional.) In any case, I highly recommend both power trim and power tilt for motors larger than 40 horsepower.

Incidentally, Southeastern Marine makes a neat power trim control that fits onto the handle of the speed control lever of some motors. Called E-Z Trim, this device permits the angler to adjust the trim without taking his hands away from either the throttle or the steering wheel.

Electric starters. Some of the smaller bass boats are operated by manual start motors (or can be), but these are not nearly as convenient as electric starters. Most motors from 20 horsepower on up have electric starters either as standard or optional. Electric starter kits are also available for some motors under 20 horsepower.

Electric starters are considerably more expensive than manual starters. At the time of this writing, for example, the suggested retail price of an Evinrude 40-horsepower motor is $915; the same motor with an electric starter is $1050. The electric starter is worth the extra $135, though, if you fish a lot. I know one bass angler who had a heart attack while trying to crank a 55-horsepower manual start outboard!

Remote steering. A bass boat needs a remote steering system, either of the console or stick type. As discussed in the last chapter, the type of steering used depends on the design of the boat. A few two-seaters, however, can be steered manually from the rear fishing seat; but it is uncomfortable to steer a motor from a high pedestal seat. If the economy-minded bass angler does try manual steering, the motor's tiller handle should have a long shaft or a shaft extension handle, and the rear seat should be off center by 6 or 8 inches. The best bet, however, is to install stick steering beside the front fishing seat.

Tachometers and speedometers. Both tachometers and speedometers are worthwhile, especially with large motors. Speedometers work with any boat, and tachometers are available for most motors of 20 horsepower on up. These instruments help the boater find the most efficient engine speed, trim position, and propeller. Few anglers realize it, but the prop that comes on a motor might not be ideal for their bass boat. The only way to check prop efficiency is to use a tachometer.

If you're interested in props, write Evinrude for a copy of their Propeller Manual, which is free as long as they last. A good marine dealer can also help you with propeller problems, but to make any meaningful tests he'll have to use a tachometer.

Service manual. Anglers who want to repair or tune up their outboard should buy a service manual, which is much more detailed than the owner's manual. They usually cost about $4.00, and are well worth it. Up until the last few years, I had a thing about outboard motors, and felt that they didn't like me or didn't understand me. The problem was that I didn't understand them.

Kill switch. This device, to be discussed more fully in Chapter 12, is designed to cut the engine off in case the bass boat operator is thrown from his seat. They cost only a few dollars, take only a few minutes to install, and could save your life.

After a friend read my book *Fishing for Bass,* he commented that bass boats sounded like something out of NASA. He wasn't being face-tious, but there is some basis for a grin or two. Some bass anglers are putting everything imaginable on their rigs, and manufacturers are offering a seemingly endless selection of options, accessories, and gadgets. Stereo tape decks—with tapes of a bass pro giving advice. CB radios and "walkie-talkies." Drink holders. Sunshades that attach to pedestal seats. Courtesy lights. Even electric fans that operate from a 12-volt boat battery!

Still, there are some very good accessories and gear for bass boats. In addition to the fishing aids discussed in Part 2 and the safety devices discussed in Chapter 12, here are some accessories that are pretty much standard on the complete bassman's boat:

Batteries, chargers, and voltmeters. All bass boats require at least one battery; and it's a good idea to have at least two on boats with large motors, so that the battery used with the electric motor and electronic gear doesn't have to operate the starter motor on the main engine.

I prefer heavy-duty marine batteries, but many bass anglers get by nicely with regular automobile batteries. The main thing is that the angler get a good, powerful battery. It should be at least 80 ampere-hours. Small batteries, such as those used on motorcycles, *can* be used to operate electric motors when size and weight are important, but, of course, they don't last very long under hard fishing.

Whatever battery you use, it should be kept clean, full of water, and properly charged. One of the worst things you can do to a wet-cell bat-tery is let it sit for long periods in an uncharged state, especially in hot weather; lead sulphate forms in the battery, and it keeps the chemicals from going back into solution. The next worst thing you can do is to overcharge the battery. Overcharging causes the battery to get too hot, thereby destroying the grid work.

There are a number of good battery chargers on the market, and most of them do an effective job if they are properly used. I prefer a 12-ampere charger with an automatic shutoff circuit, which prevents overcharging and consequent overheating. My second choice would be a little 3-ampere "trickle" charger, which won't overdo the job too much if I should forget and leave it on for 24 hours.

Many of the larger bass boats have the batteries more or less fixed in a closed compartment. On some boats, however, the battery will be loose on the deck, in which case it is a good idea to purchase a waterproof polyethylene battery box. Good ones protect the battery from the elements and offer a degree of protection from acid in case the battery should turn over.

Battery charge indicators, or voltmeters, are available for mounting on an instrument panel. They are nice to have, but aren't entirely necessary. I do, however, recommend that the angler check the battery with a hydrometer from time to time to make certain that the charger is bringing it up to full power.

Anchors. Every boat needs at least one anchor, and bass boats need two so that the angler can position the boat precisely in relation to underwater structure. Each anchor should have at least 50 feet of line. I prefer 15-pound mushroom anchors that are made of lead and coated with rubber or vinyl. They are less noisy than anchors made of cast iron or other metal.

Most bass anglers prefer some sort of winch system for raising the anchor, and bass boats are usually rigged with anchor reel and bow mount. The reel releases the anchor when the control button is turned (or pushed), and the anchor is retrieved by cranking the handle clockwise. When not in use, the anchor is stored in a "davit" housing so that it is ready for instant use. One problem that I have encountered from time to time is that the anchor sometimes sticks or binds in the housing and has to be loosened by hand before it will drop.

Several firms market electric anchor windlass units, and I was quickly spoiled by my LectrAnchor. Electric anchors save some time and muscle, but the main advantage (at least to me) is that they permit a lone angler to get the anchor and rope out of the water when he ties into a real lunker. Another advantage is that the better electric anchors are quieter than manual winch systems. The anchor is raised or lowered by toggle switches, which can be operated by hand or foot, and the rate at which the anchor drops is controlled by the motor. I might add that far too many inexperienced anglers let the anchor splash into the

Electric anchors are becoming more popular on bass boats. On this model, the electric motor is mounted under the decking. Note the toggle switches.

water and don't check its fall to the bottom. A 15-pound anchor hitting bottom is certain to make a thud that bass can hear for long distances.

Some of the better electric anchors retail at about $150, which is a sizable investment for many of us. But I think they are worth the money to anyone who does a lot of bass fishing in deep water. The angler who almost always fishes the bank or visible cover, however, really doesn't need one if he has a foot-controlled electric motor.

In addition to the Johnny Reb LectrAnchor, other electric anchors are made by Motor-Guide, Dutton-Lainson Company, Reel Power, Ram-Glas, and possibly other firms. Write the manufacturers for further information. As I indicated, I haven't investigated the operation of all these anchor systems, but most of them are probably good. Before buying one, make sure that you can mount it conveniently on your boat; some have the complete unit above the deck, but others are designed so that the motor is below deck. I would also take a close look at the mount or "davit" housing. The smoothest and quietest ones that I have ever used had nylon rollers and were designed to prevent metal-to-anchor contact.

Live wells and aerators. Any bassman who wants to keep his catch, or part of it, should have a good live well on his boat. Fish stringers will do on the smaller boats on which a large live well might clutter things up too much, but any bass that is to be kept and later released fares better in an oxygenated live well. Live wells and oxygenating aerators are, in fact, standard gear on bass boats used in some tournaments where bonus points are given for each bass that survives.

There are a number of aerators on the market. Most of them use the 12-volt battery as a power source, but a few use flashlight batteries.

There are two basic types of aerators. The first operates by pumping air bubbles into the water (as in a small home aquarium). The others operate by jetting streams of water into the live well, and this type seems to have become the choice of tournament anglers (and of bait dealers who must keep thousands of minnows and shiners alive and well). Several firms market jet spray aerators, and most of them can be used with a permanent live well or with a large ice chest. All of these units have a submergible pump that circulates water from the live well (or ice chest), through suitable piping, and jets it back down into the live well from the top. They can also be used as emergency bilge pumps.

Personally, I could get along fine without either a live well or an ice chest aerator, but they are almost essential if you plan to fish in tournaments that stress keeping your catch alive so that they can be released after they are weighed in. I don't have an extensive list of aerator manufacturers. The best bet would be to consult with your marine dealer, or consult the catalogs published by Bassmaster Pro Shops, Bass Pro Shops, and Okiebug. You might also check with firms

that supply equipment to bait dealers; their addresses can be found
in the classified ad sections of the large national outdoor magazines.

Rod racks. Most bass boats come equipped with one or more rod
racks, or have them available as options. Some have enclosed rod
storage compartments on either side of the boat; I like these because
they can be locked up, and one can leave his rods in them at all times.
Newcomers to the sport of bass angling might wonder why some
boats are rigged with the capacity to hold so many rods. Well, it's
because a lot of bassmen carry along five or six rods and reels of one
sort or another, rigged with lines of various weights and with lures
of different types, sizes, and colors. This saves them a lot of time when
they're switching from one lure or line weight to another. If two anglers each have five rods on the same bass boat, rod racks are almost
necessary to keep things straight and uncluttered.

Apart from factory-installed rod compartments, the angler has a
wide choice of racks that can be mounted in bass boats. Another handy
item to have on a bass boat is a rod tender, which is simply a plastic
pipe that mounts to the side of the boat and holds the rod in a vertical position. These aren't recommended for holding a rod when you're
running the boat at high speed, and they don't work too well for
holding one rod while you're fishing with another, but they are nice
and noiseless for holding the rod while you change lures or pour yourself a cup of coffee. They are especially useful in bass boats that have
carpet on the decking; the reason is that if you put the rod down while
a lure is attached to the line, you may spend the next 15 minutes
trying to get hooks out of the carpet.

Ambassadeur fans might be interested in a custom-tailored rod
holder for the 5000 and 6000 reels. Called the Quick Draw rod holder,
it eliminates the need for forcing the rod into clamps of one sort or
another. Neat.

12

Safety Features and Devices

As MORE AND MORE bass boats zip faster and faster up and down lakes and impoundments from coast to coast, it becomes increasingly clear that they are not safe. Although the boat itself—construction, flotation, etc.—should be considered from a safety viewpoint, the big problem is not with the boat as such. Most of the reputable bass boats are well designed and adequately made these days; some of them will float even if cut in half, and they are quite stable.

I do, however, feel that some of the deck-mounted pedestal seats are far too high. No doubt the manufacturers will tell you that the pedestals support *fishing* seats and that they should be vacated for high-speed running. But I've seen a number of anglers riding high at full speed. They are asking for trouble. Sitting that high out of the water raises the center of gravity and makes the boat easy to capsize either when running at high speed, from the wake of another craft, or in choppy water. The biggest danger, however, is of the angler being thrown head over heels if the boat suddenly decelerates for one reason or another. It is simply a matter of leverage, and a high seat works something like a catapult if the boat is suddenly stopped.

Pedestal fishing seats are too high out of the water on some boats to be used at high speeds. These two anglers know where to sit.

I also feel that bass boats have steadily become too powerful for the angler's own good. The horsepower craze has come about at least partly because of the demands of tournament fishing, in which the contestants, understandably, don't want to lose a minute while going from one hot spot to another. Indeed, the initial run from the starting line to fishing areas resembles a race. I am, however, happy to report that B.A.S.S. and other large tournament organizations have now limited the horsepower on contestants' boats, owing in part to the energy crisis and in part to safety considerations. As of this writing, the B.A.S.S. tournaments allow motors no larger than the U.S. Coast Guard's approved rating for a particular boat. According to the Coast Guard ruling, all new boats must have a horsepower rating stamped onto a metal plate, and the plate must be affixed to the hull. For the 16-foot Ranger bass boats that have been used in some B.A.S.S. tournaments, for example, the approved rating is 85 horsepower, whereas many anglers have used (and still do) 135-horsepower motors on comparable 16-foot boats. It's my opinion that the Coast Guard ratings ought to be enforced in each state.

Anglers with other opinions might point out that ski boats and pleasure craft are often powered by large engines without a very high accident rate. Maybe. But they are not *fishing* boats. For one thing, the seats are lower. For another, they don't as often run full speed through prime bass fishing areas of large impoundments; a big percentage of the pleasure boats operate on large natural lakes or in open water areas of impoundments. There are exceptions, I'm sure, with individuals and with locale, but statistically speaking a ski boat isn't as likely to hit a stump or other underwater obstruction.

Although a number of boating mishaps occur in natural lakes and in rivers, the impoundments are much more dangerous because of flooded timber. One big problem is that the timber eventually rots at the waterline. Falling tops can be a hazard, especially in windy weather, but the standing stump is much more dangerous over the long run. This problem is complicated because the water level fluctuates quite a lot in many impoundments. Consequently, the stumps

Submerged timber often makes for excellent bass fishing, as shown by this stringer from Toledo Bend. But it also creates boating hazards.

are not all equidistant from the surface. At a certain pool elevation, the tops of some stumps may be 5 feet out of the water, others barely under the surface, and still others 5 feet deep. Thus, a boating route might be perfectly safe one month and dangerous the next.

Hitting a stump and merely being thrown overboard isn't the whole story. Nor is drowning. The worst hazard is that once the angler is thrown overboard at high speed the boat might well recover and keep going. The propeller creates a torque, which causes the boat to run in a circle. Thus, the drenched angler finds the boat coming at him. He can usually get out of the way, but it keeps coming back time after time, until it runs out of gas. An alarming number of anglers have either been chopped up by boat propellers or have had narrow escapes. For example, a young couple were thrown from their boat while fishing in a tournament on Toledo Bend. Her arm was severed and she bled to death in the water. He was crippled for life.

Clearly, some impoundments—and certainly specific areas of them —are no place for high-speed boats. Period. And too many anglers run too fast in bass waters, either from ignorance or from foolishness, or both.

In addition to buying a well-made boat and running it at a reasonable speed, the bassman can take certain precautions to help insure safe fishing. He can keep his boat shipshape, make sure that his motor stays in good repair, and keep a close eye on the linkage mechanisms in his steering system. He can also make sure that he has life jackets and other safety devices aboard in good condition. Some of these devices are required by federal and state laws. The federal laws are enforced by the U.S. Coast Guard, which has jurisdiction over navigable streams (and associated impoundments) that flow into the oceans. The Coast Guard also has jurisdiction over any body of water that borders two or more states. Whether or not the following items are required by law, the bassman should give them some consideration:

Kill switches. One of the most important safety devices for bass boats is the kill switch, designed to break the ignition circuit in case the boat operator is thrown from the wheel. This, of course, shuts off the motor and thereby precludes injury from the props of a loose boat. Although kill switches are not 100 percent foolproof, they are highly desirable safety features, and they are now required on bass boats used in some tournaments.

There are several types of kill switches, operated either by foot or automatically when the operator is thrown from his seat. Mercury, Chrysler, Johnson, and Evinrude offer kill switches, and others are marketed by various small firms such as Little Beaver. Most marine dealers now stock them, and some install them on new bass boats. A temporary kill switch can be made simply by tying a cord to an ignition wire and attaching the other end of the cord to your belt so that if you are thrown overboard the wire will break and kill the motor. If you should be thrown overboard, you'll later have to splice the wire back together, but that's better than having a prop chew you up.

Some kill switches operate by a contact activation device in the driver's seat. When pressure is applied, contact is made and the motor will start and run. When the pressure is removed, the motor can't be started or will shut off if it is already running. This is a neat design, but the operator must remember what he is sitting on. If he should raise up for some reason, such as to adjust the gain control on his depth finder, the engine will shut off and the deceleration itself could throw him overboard. Foot-operated switches can also be triggered accidentally. Personally, I prefer the lanyard type that attach to the operator's clothing or to his belt.

Until recently, all the kill switches were electrical and their installation required splicing into the boat's wiring. OMC has, however, recently come out with a completely mechanical system, in which a lanyard turns the ignition key off if the operator should be thrown. The key is left in the switch, so that the motor can be restarted by another party in the boat. The device fits Evinrude and Johnson outboards as well as OMC stern drive units. Kits are available for Mercury and Chrysler outboards.

Life preservers. The U.S. Coast Guard approves four types of personal flotation devices, and the boater should not purchase a life preserver unless the label states that it has been approved by the Coast Guard.

Type I designates wearable life preservers with more than 20 pounds of buoyancy, designed to turn an unconscious person so that he is not face down in the water; Type II is the same except that the preserver must have at least 15.5 pounds of buoyancy. Type III designates wearable life preservers with 15.5 pounds of buoyancy, designed to keep a conscious person afloat; in other words, a Type III device won't necessarily turn an unconscious person upright. Type IV designates any flotation device with at least 16.5 pounds of buoyancy that is designed to be thrown instead of worn; these are the familiar doughnut-shaped lifesavers and flotation cushions.

Approved flotation cushions meet Coast Guard requirements for boats under 16 feet long. Boats over 16 feet must have at least one Type I, II, or III flotation device aboard for each person, and must

Comfortable, attractive life jackets and vests are now approved by the U.S. Coast Guard. The angler on the right, in the high fishing seat, is wearing a closed-cell foam vest.

have at least one throwable Type IV available for ready use. In all cases, flotation devices should be at hand and should not be stored in compartments with lids.

Regardless of the type of flotation device you prefer, buy good ones. Most of the buoyant cushions and inexpensive life jackets are filled with kapok, which is usually sealed in plastic bags. Most such boat cushions mat after a little use, and thereby lose at least some of their flotation properties. Kapok cushions should be replaced often if they are subjected to hard use. Also, the plastic encasing the kapok cracks or tears, so the kapok can quickly become sogged with water.

I strongly suspect that many of the plastic bags used in buoyant cushions and life jackets are not waterproof even when they are brand-new. I've bought a number of such life jackets—Coast Guard approved —that have quickly become waterlogged when my kids (or neighbors' kids) used them for playing in the water. I realize that a life jacket should not be used for playing, but the fact remains that they became sogged with water. Soggy cushions or jackets have to be discarded because there is no way to dry them out. My objection to kapok flotation devices, then, is not only to the material itself but also to the plastic bags.

In my opinion, the best material for life preservers is a good foam made from either polyethylene or polyvinyl chloride. This material, which resembles foam rubber, will not become waterlogged and doesn't mat as readily as kapok.

As already stated, the Type III jackets will not upright an unconscious person, but they may well be the best choice for bassmen to use in cooler weather. They are available as vests and jackets (and even jump suits) designed for comfort as well as flotation. Indeed, some of them are quite stylish. The better ones, which can cost $50 or more, are made with strips of soft foam covered with strong fabric. The foam slabs are contoured for comfortable fits, and many of them are indeed so comfortable that owners often use them for all-around jackets.

The foam is excellent insulation material, which makes the jackets and vests ideal for cold-weather fishing. Note that the foam will also provide a degree of insulation even if the wearer is in the water, and this can be *very* important in cold weather. Research has shown that the body must have an "inner core" temperature of a certain level if the brain and heart are to function properly. Any time the inner core temperature drops below 91 degrees F, consciousness may become hazy. At 81 degrees, the individual is in great danger. The colder the water, the quicker the body's inner core temperature drops. By the way, swimming in cold water actually reduces the body's natural insulation because it increases the flow of blood to the arms and legs, and the blood acts like a heat conductor, or heat carrier, resulting in faster body-heat depletion. Another reason is that swimming keeps the body in contact with "new" water that has not been warmed by body heat. If you are afloat in water colder than 77 degrees F, it may be better to stay put instead of trying to swim for long distances. For more on this subject, including a discussion of hypothermia and the dangerous "after-drop" phenomenon that occurs after a person is removed from cold water, write Stearns for a copy of their booklet "About Life Jackets . . . 'n PFD's."

The law does not require that life jackets be worn at all times, and too many anglers (including myself) don't like to wear Type I and II jackets in any kind of weather. But it's a very good idea to put them on while the boat is being run at high speed, and while you're fishing at night.

Fire extinguishers. Fiberglass boats will burn, and apparently do burn often enough to warrant federal and state laws. Although small fiberglass boats with outboard motors are not required by federal law to carry fire extinguishers, some states *do* require that all power boats have fire extinguishers aboard. Anyhow, fire extinguishers should be carried on bass boats whether or not they are required.

There are several types of extinguishers, designed to fight different kinds of fire. The boater should get a Type B extinguisher because it is best for flammable liquids. (Type A is recommended for common combustible materials such as wood or paper; Type C, for electrical fires, which should be extinguished with a nonconduction agent.) And remember that a fire extinguisher is worthless unless it is kept charged. I prefer those that have pressure gauges and that can be recharged.

Although a few boats equipped with outboard motors have no doubt burned up, the biggest danger is from boats with inboard engines. The problem is that vapor can get trapped somewhere below deck, and a spark will set it off. (Not long ago, for example, a boat exploded behind my house one night, then caught fire, burned, and sank.) In addition to having one or more fire extinguishers aboard, boats with inboard motors should have properly placed ventilation ducts and backfire flame arresters. Bass boats with enclosed fuel tanks also require proper ventilation. If in doubt about your boat, write the Coast Guard (400 Seventh Street, S.W., Washington, D.C. 20591) for a copy of their booklet "Ventilation Systems for Small Craft."

Anchors. The sudden release of a bow anchor can cause boating mishaps. I am currently using a LectrAnchor that has a strong safety-pin lock for keeping the anchor in place for trailering and while running in rough water. If you use either a manual or electric winch system that doesn't have some sort of safety locking device, it would be a good idea to install a safety pin or some other means of securing the bow anchor for high-speed running. (Safety pins can also be installed on stern-mounted anchors, but these are not as likely to cause an accident if they should drop down at high speeds.) In case you (or your boat dealer) can't figure out a good locking device, you can always put the anchor into the boat for high-speed running.

Anyhow, some states require that boats have at least one anchor aboard.

Polarized glasses. It's my opinion that good polarized glasses make boating a little safer in fishing. In addition to helping the boater see obstructions better, polarized glasses cut glare on the surface so that stickups can be spotted sooner. Also, studies have shown that good sunglasses worn during the fishing trip help prevent eyestrain, so that the angler's automobile drive back home after dark is safer.

Compass. It's easy to get lost on a large body of water after dark or in heavy fog. Not long ago, for example, a fellow knocked on my door about midnight. As it turned out, he had been lost here on Lake Weir since about sundown, and he wanted to use our telephone to call his wife to come after him. He had to have our address, and he couldn't believe it when we told him that we lived on Bird Island. His house was only a short distance away, on Bird Island Road. He had thought that he was all the way across the lake in Oklawaha. A compass could have kept him straight. So, get a good one and learn how to use it.

Whistles or horns. Federal laws require that small boats carry a whistle or a horn that can be heard for at least half a mile.

Lights. Federal laws and most state laws require that a boat have navigation lights. Boats under 26 feet long must have running lights on the bow—a green one on the starboard side and a red one on the port side. They must also have a white light, usually mounted on the stern, for use when the boat is anchored. It is also a good idea to have a strong searchlight aboard—but keep it shut off while you are fishing for bass. A strong searchlight is a good thing to have for running in bass waters, but they'll scare a bass half to death, especially in shallow water.

Paddles. If a bass fisherman has his boat rigged with an electric motor, as he surely should have, paddles aren't often used for fishing purposes. But it's a good idea to take one along, just in case you need it. In some states, paddles are required by law.

Bailer. Some sort of bilge pump or bailer should be aboard every boat. A permanently mounted electric bilge pump is the best bet, but a two-pound coffee can, slightly bent at the mouth, will usually be sufficient. Check the laws in your state.

First aid kits. Keep a good first aid kit tucked away somewhere in a storage compartment, and remember to replace items that have been used.

Flares. If you fish in very large lakes, impoundments, or rivers, a red flare kit might come in handy in case you have motor trouble or get caught out for one reason or another. Compact kits are available and don't take up much room.

Hitting stumps and other obstructions in the water is the most common cause of serious accidents involving bass boats on impoundments. The next most common cause is probably the failure of the steering linkage system, either through improper installation or because the linkage system was not adequate for the motor being used on the boat.

In the May/June 1974 *BASSmaster Magazine,* Chuck Garrison reported some good advice and tips from Officer Lysle Gray of the U.S. Coast Guard's Boating Standards Division:

> Officer Gray explains that among the steering linkage problems which can occur, a slip joint can vibrate loose, an improperly selected pivot point in the linkage anchoring system can break away or if the steering linkage is improperly installed near the motor, the motor's lower unit can strike a submerged object and send the motor flipping upward, tearing loose any linkage it may strike.
>
> To guard against such mishaps, Gray recommends that bass anglers inspect their rigs when they are bought, and before being launched.
>
> "Check all of the steering system bolts for tightness, then recheck them again after the first couple of hours of use," he

cautions. After that, the steering system should be rechecked periodically.

Other safeguards against accidents suggested by Gray include (1) securing all vital nuts from backing off by using proper lock washers and/or double nuts; (2) using small hose clamps to help back up springs or other sliding connections which are part of the steering linkage mechanism; (3) peening steering nuts with a hammer or drilling a hole through the bolt and securing the nut from backing off by the use of a cotter pin. Also, the motor should be brought up to full-tilt position to make sure it does not hit any part of the steering linkage.

To Gordon Holland of Tulsa, Oklahoma, it was a problem with the stick steering type of installation that gave him a close call with possible serious injury or even death. Holland, who is assistant sales manager with Lowrance Electronics, the maker of the now famous "little green box" Fish Lo-K-Tor, was competing in a local bass club tourney last year on Lake Oologah in northeastern Oklahoma. He had a good catch in progress and was thinking about the prospects of taking home a trophy as he moved at full throttle to the next fishing spot.

"About 45 seconds after starting out, I sensed the stick steering lever felt loose," Holland related. "It wasn't drastically loose, but I knew something didn't feel right."

Reacting quickly, he pulled the throttle backward. When the throttle was half-way back, the stick handle to the steering unit came off in his hand and the boat skirted into an abrupt 360-degree spin. He was lucky. He threw the throttle all the way back, bringing the boat to a stop while he held on tightly to keep from being pitched out. He escaped injury.

The article (and Officer Gray) makes it clear that most failures in steering systems are not the result of faulty design or manufacture, but of improper *installation*. It's my opinion that boat dealers, or manufacturers who install steering systems at the factory, ought to be held liable for negligence if they install a steering system improperly or inadequately. Sue the bastards.

13

Other Boats
for
Bass Fishing

Before proceeding with a discussion of some small boats, maybe I
had better state that I think the fully rigged bass boat is the greatest
fishing aid since the rod and reel. It allows a bassman to fish quite
comfortably for long periods of time, and this results in his making
more casts, and more effective casts, during a hard day's fishing. Also,
the bass boat is clearly more suitable than a canoe for fishing in large
impoundments, where white-capping water isn't uncommon; and the
bass boat can transport the angler quickly from one hot spot to another, often miles apart.

While the bassmen are riding high up and down the large impoundments, however, a lot of anglers are taking limits of bass on smaller
or less sophisticated boats, often in ponds, remote lakes, or small
streams. Some of these anglers are of another breed of bassmen. Often
loners, they don't like to fish around water skiers or even other anglers, and I suspect that they might well account for more than their
share of really large bass.

I like both kinds of fishing, but if I were fishing exclusively for a world's record bass, I doubt that I would use a fancy bass boat. I would probably find myself a weathered old cypress boat with a low profile, and I would rig it for silent running. But the point I want to make is that the angler who doesn't own a $7,000 bass boat should not feel that he can't catch bass, and lots of them. In fact, the larger bass boats, especially those with high deck-mounted pedestal seats, may even be undesirable on some remote ponds, lakes, and streams. Looking back on my angling experiences, I feel that some of the most memorable times were on small streams, and this is a pleasure that many bassmen will never know unless they get themselves a small boat.

Almost any small boat will do for bass fishing, provided that the angler picks his time and place carefully. The middle of a 100-mile-long impoundment, of course, is no place for a 10-foot johnboat; any wind at all coming down the channel will make the water too choppy for pleasant fishing, and could well be dangerous. A small boat, on the other hand, might be perfectly safe on some quiet cove of the same impoundment.

Here are some types of small and more or less inexpensive boats suitable for off-the-beaten-path bass fishing, together with what I consider to be their advantages and disadvantages:

Johnboats. For a long time now, the flat-bottomed, square-end johnboats have been popular among many bass anglers. They are light and inexpensive, and their flat shape makes them easy to car-top. Although the early johnboats were made of wood, most of the modern ones are aluminum. The big disadvantage of aluminum is that it is noisy, and anyone using an aluminum boat will improve his catch by taking extra pains to be quiet. Even shutting the lid of a tackle box seems to make a lot of noise in an aluminum boat. Still, the aluminum johnboat is, in my opinion, the best design for bass anglers who can't afford big bass boats. The square bow and flat bow deck makes them readily adaptable to foot-controlled electric motors and other bass boat accessories. I might add that fishing decks of marine plywood can be mounted on the front of large johnboats; also, swivel seats can be mounted on the cross seats, although these aren't quite as comfortable as pedestal fishing seats. I've seen a couple of 16-foot johnboats that were really rigged up for bass fishing.

The johnboat is a shallow-draft design, which makes it a good choice for fishing in weed beds and similar cover, but its lack of depth

Using just a johnboat and a paddle, these anglers have tied into a nice bass on Cow Pen Bayou, Louisiana.

—the sides aren't very high—makes the 10- or 12-foot length a dubious choice for choppy water. But it is great for small ponds and some streams.

Semi-vees. Typically, these boats have a pointed bow, a square stern, and a rather rounded bottom. Most of them are deeper than johnboats of comparable length. Made of aluminum or fiberglass, the boat may be a good choice for general use, but, in my opinion, it is rather limited for bass fishing because the pointed bow makes it difficult to mount a foot-controlled electric motor, and the rounded deck on the front part of some semi-vee boats makes it awkward to mount, and use, a foot pedal. In short, the semi-vee boat is not as versatile as the johnboat; but most models have more depth than johnboats, which makes them more suitable for choppy water.

These Florida anglers take a nice bass from a semi-vee boat.

Canoes. Although canoeing is a great sport, it is my opinion that the canoe itself is not an ideal fishing platform, and casting for long periods of time from a canoe is rather tiring. On the other hand, the typical canoe is light and maneuverable, qualities that make it a good choice for fishing small streams. It is also a good choice for anglers who don't have gasoline or electric motors, or who like to fish remote spots; it is an easy craft to paddle, and makes for relatively easy portage.

Almost all canoes these days are made from either fiberglass or aluminum. Aluminum canoes are usually lighter, but they are also much more noisy. A few canoes are molded from foam material, but I don't think these are durable enough for bass fishing.

My personal choice in a canoe is the ultralight job made from aircraft aluminum and lined with foam to deaden noise. Sportspal and Norcal (a Canadian firm) make these canoes, and Sears markets one that is probably made by either Sportspal or Norcal. The 14-foot Sears boat weighs only 48 pounds, and the 12-foot Sportspal weighs less than 30 pounds! Such light weight makes these canoes ideal for fishing small streams where the angler must frequently go around, or over, fallen trees and logs. On the other hand, these canoes are not recommended for use in whitewater streams because rocks can easily damage their thin hulls. (So can hard knots on seemingly rotten pine logs!) Heavier canoes made from marine aluminum are better for swift, rocky streams.

A number of canoe manufacturers make square stern models for use with small outboards (or electrics), and most other canoes can be fitted with motor mounts that will permit the use of small motors on the side of the rear end. A lot of anglers use the side mounts for electrics, and I suspect that fitting such a mount on the bow end of the boat, but within easy reach of the front seat, will give the angler more control and maneuverability. In my opinion, however, a large battery isn't quite compatible with the canoe, although some electrics will operate nicely from a small 6-volt automobile battery or even a motorcycle battery.

Most canoes are 14 feet long or so, but 17-footers are not uncommon. A recent trend, however, is toward small one-man canoes of about 10 feet, and these are great for fishing small streams.

The neatest rig I've seen for fishing creeks and small ponds is a little boat that my nephew designed. Called Stump Knocker, it's an 11-foot fiberglass canoelike craft with a pointed bow and a contoured stern squared off to take an electric motor. It doesn't have slat seats. Instead, the angler sits astride the cushioned top of an elongated live well and storage box running down the center of the boat. This unusual seating arrangement seems to help the angler keep his balance. It's a neat design, and is the only tiny boat I've ever seen with a built-in live well. Although he is more craftsman than manufacturer, I have listed Stump Knocker in the directory in Part Four because I think the design is unique.

Bass bugs. I've seen several models of tiny one-man fishing rigs that consist of a single seat on a rather square little platform, as shown in the accompanying photograph. On some of these, the platform has a mount for an electric motor, and the battery fits neatly under the fisherman's seat. I like the idea of a quiet little craft of this type, but they are rather top-heavy and shouldn't be used in choppy water—or far from shore. Nor are they ideal for fishing in streams; their rather blunt lines and blocky shape makes them difficult to maneuver in swift water. They are, though, great for fishing in small ponds. The high seat, which is often molded to shape, makes them more comfortable for casting than canoes or tubes.

Who needs a big bass boat? This Texas angler uses a tiny bass bug.

On some bass bugs, the angler sits with his feet dangling in the water and can use scuba diver's fins on his feet for propulsion. This design is more stable than the others, since the angler sits lower. The disadvantages of this design are that the angler has to get his feet wet and that bow-mounted electric motors can't be used with them, unless the angler wants to risk sticking his big toe into the prop from time to time.

Tubes. Automotive-type inner tubes fitted with a canvas cover and saddle seat have for a long time been used for bass fishing. They are fine for fishing small ponds, and they are not as tippy as canoes or bass bugs because the angler's feet and legs (up to his waist) are in the water. Some anglers move about by paddling with their hands and kicking with their feet, but paddle flippers can be obtained. These buckle onto the angler's foot and are designed so that the fins fold in on the forward stroke and then flip out on the backward stroke, thereby permitting the angler to "walk" through the water.

This South Dakota angler uses a tube. Note the rod-holder attachment.

Some of the canvas covers have some sort of built-in rod holder (which is needed) and a tackle compartment.

Inflatable boats. The familiar rubber life rafts were the first inflatable boats, and the early ones left a lot to be desired. They rotted, for one thing. In recent years, however, inflatables have shown marked improvements, owing largely to new synthetic materials. Modern inflatables are tough; in fact, they are used to shoot rapids, and the better ones are virtually unsinkable because they have separate air chambers. They are, of course, easy to haul around in the trunk of a car, which, in my opinion, is their main advantage.

But, unfortunately, they are not ideal for bass fishing. Although some of them have transom-mount motors, using an electric off the bow is virtually impossible. Moreover, the inflatables are difficult to paddle and maneuver because of their basic life-raft shape. A few models, however, are rather canoe-shaped, and these are more suitable for bass fishing. One very good feature of inflatables is that they are less noisy than aluminum, fiberglass, or wooden boats. That means a lot when you're after bass! If some manufacturer would make a model with comfortable seats and a bow deck for mounting an electric motor, I'd get one for sure.

Part Four

Tackle
and
Boat Companies

Tackle
and
Boat Companies

Abercrombie & Fitch Company, P.O. Box 4288, Grand Central Station, New York, New York 10017. Fine things for anglers and other outdoorsmen. Catalog available.

Tony Accetta & Son, Inc., 932 Avenue E, Riviera Beach, Florida 33404. Spin Dodger, jigs, and other lures. I like Accetta spoons because the firm markets replacement hooks and weed guards for them.

Acme Tackle Company, 69 Bucklin Street, Providence, Rhode Island 02907. Fiord and other spoons.

Aitken-Warner Corporation, 427 Beech Street, Green Camp, Ohio 43322. Warner's soft plastic lures, Krazy Minnow spoons, and other baits.

Aladdin Manufacturing Company, P.O. Box 97, Friars Point, Mississippi 38631. Bass boats.

Allan Manufacturing Company, 325 Duffy Avenue, Hicksville, Long Island, New York 11801. Allan makes a wide variety of tips, guides, and other rod hardware, along with a few rod holders and other gear. The firm has recently introduced a new "ceramic" guide made of titanium dioxide, which is their answer to aluminum oxide.

Allied Sports, One Humminbird Lane, Eufaula, Alabama 36027. Humminbird depth finders.

Allison Craft Boats, Route 1, Louisville, Tennessee 37777. Bass boats. Apparently Allison was the first firm to feature high-performance hulls on bass boats.

America's Cup, Inc., 1109 South Fremont Street, Alhambra, California 91803. Flotation vests and life jackets, featuring closed-cell vinyl foam. One of their vests is used in the Bassmaster Classic tournament.

AMF Crestline Division, 609 13th Avenue, N.E., Little Falls, Minnesota 56345. Bass boats.

Ande, Inc., 1500 53rd Street, West Palm Beach, Florida 33407. Exclusive importers of Ande monofilament fishing line, which is popular with charter boat skippers and saltwater anglers. Ande line has landed more than 48 world-record fish, including the largest fish ever caught on monofilament—a 1,218-pound black marlin, taken on 80-pound line. According to a spokesman for the firm, a bass angler using 20-pound Ande line on Lake Okeechobee hooked into a bass but thought he had a whale. What he finally landed was a 7-pound bass and a car radiator!

Appleby Manufacturing Company, Interstate 44, Lebanon, Missouri 65536. Bass boats.

AquaBug International, Inc., P.O. Box 61, Lawrence, New York 11559. This firm makes a tiny 11-pound outboard motor, which runs up to 24 hours on a gallon of gas.

Aqua Meter Instrument Corporation, 465 Eagle Rock Avenue, Roseland, New Jersey 07068. Aqua Meter depth finders (flashers) with removable sun shields; some models designed to be mounted on instrument panels. Compasses, marine barometers, clocks, and other instruments.

Fred Arbogast Company, Inc., 313 West North Street, Akron, Ohio 44303. Jitterbug, Hawaiian Wiggler, and other top bass catchers. Also, Hi-Tail plastic worms and Hula Popper fly rod lures. Rubber Hula skirts.

Arrowcraft, P.O. Box 700, Pearland, Texas 77581. This firm manufactures boats with fan-type propulsion, or "air boats." Their Skimmer model comes rigged with pedestal fishing seats, and looks like a propeller-driven bass boat.

Arrow Glass Boat and Manufacturing Corporation, 931 Firestone Building, Memphis, Tennessee 38107. Bass boats.

Ashaway Line & Twine Manufacturing Company, Ashaway, Rhode Island 02804. Braided lines and fly lines. Established almost 150 years ago, this firm introduced the first dacron line in 1952.

Astroglass Boat Company, P.O. Box 7, Pleasant View, Tennessee 37146. Bass boats, including two new high-performance designs with tri-vee hulls.

Jim Bagley Bait Company, P.O. Box 110, Winter Haven, Florida 33880. Plastic worms, spinnerbaits, and other lures. This firm makes the only mass-produced balsa lures in this country, with several sizes and models of the Bagley Balsa B and the Bang-O-Lure.

B & B Tackle Company, 1600 West Frank Street, Lufkin, Texas 75901. Lures and fishing accessories.

Bass Buster, Inc., P.O. Box 118, Amsterdam, Missouri 64723. Plastic worms and various spinnerbaits, including the Tarantula. Maribou jigs and a weedless (fiber guard) jig head for fishing plastic worms.

Bassmaster Pro Shop, P.O. Box 3044, Montgomery, Alabama 36109. Operated by B.A.S.S., this mail-order source offers a wide variety of lures, tackle, attire, electronic gear, and other goodies for the bassman, including the Ray Scott line of rods. Catalog available; mail orders welcome.

Bass Pro Shops, P.O. Box 441, Springfield, Missouri 65804. This large retail and mail-order house specializes in bass fishing tackle and gear. They also market their own line of spinnerbaits and other items. Large catalog available; mail orders welcome.

L. L. Bean, Inc., Freeport, Maine 04032. This delightful firm offers a line of attire and gear for fishermen and other outdoorsmen. Their fishing line is rather limited in bass gear, but they do offer such top-quality products as the Fenwick H.M.G. fly rods and the Italian Pescador spinning reels. Seasonal catalogs available. Mail orders welcome.

Berkley and Company, Highway 9 and 71, Spirit Lake, Iowa 51360. Trilene monofilament, braided lines, and fly lines. Para/Metric rods. Spinning and spincast reels. Fly reels. Berkley makes a baitcasting reel, but it is not free-spooling.

Best Tackle Manufacturing Company, 3106 Bay Street, Unionville, Michigan 48767. Homer LeBlanc's Swim Whizz, Stanley Streamer action flies, and other lures.

Betts Tackle Ltd., P.O. Box 57, Fuquay-Varina, North Carolina 27526. Spinnerbaits, jigs, and a large selection of bass bugs and flies.

Blakemore, P.O. Box 505, Branson, Missouri 65616. Twister spinnerbaits and other lures. Magnum marine batteries.

Bomber Bait Company, P.O. Box 716, Gainesville, Texas 76240. Pinfish, Waterdog, Bushwhacker spinnerbaits, Spinstick, and other lures.

Bonanza Molding Corporation, P.O. Box 788, Camdenton, Missouri 65202. Bass boats.

Bonito Boats, Inc., P.O. Box 7528, Orlando, Florida 32805. Bass boats.

Boone Bait Company, Inc., P.O. Box 571, Winter Park, Florida 32789. Touts, bass bugs, plastic worms, and other lures.

Boston Whaler, Inc., 1149 Hingham Street, Rockland, Massachusetts 02370. This firm has a good reputation for tough, well-designed fiberglass boats, but they aren't for bargain hunters. They offer a number of small boats (up to 19 feet), but so far they have only one bass model, a 16-footer.

Browning, Route 1, Morgan, Utah 84050. Silaflex casting rods, some of which have aluminum oxide guides and tips. Also, rod blanks and handles. Spinning, spincast, and fly reels. I've recently tested some Browning fishing gear, and the quality seems to be as high as that of their shotguns; they don't, however, break their necks catering to bass anglers. If their tackle division would make a baitcasting reel, and if their marine division would make a bass boat. . . .

Buck's Baits, P.O. Box 66, Hickory, North Carolina 28601. Spoonplugs and trolling gear by Buck Perry, said to be the grandfather of structure fishing.

Gene Bullard Custom Rods, 10139 Shoreview Road, Dallas, Texas 75238. Custom rods; graphite blanks and other rod-building materials. Name-brand tackle and lures. Mail-order catalog available.

Burke Fishing Lures, 1969 South Airport Road, Traverse City, Michigan 49684. Buckshot worms and other soft plastic lures. Spinnerbaits, jigs, and plugs.

Byrd Industries, Inc., 201 Rock Industrial Park Drive, Bridgeton, Missouri 63044. Lazi-Trol electric motors. Battery chargers and various electric motor mounting brackets.

California Tackle Company, Inc., 430 West Redondo Beach Boulevard, Gardena, California 90284. Sabre rod blanks. Guides, tips, butt caps, and other rod components.

C & G Tackle Manufacturing Company, P.O. Box 1402, Tulsa, Oklahoma 74101. Heavy-duty fish stringers made with a brass chain encased in plastic and with stainless steel "safety lock" hooks. I said some bad things about safety-pin stringers in my book *Fishing for Bass.* The C & G stringers force me to take it all back! There's not a bass alive that can straighten out one of C & G's safety-pin hooks.

Cape Cod Line Company, Division of Brownell & Company, Inc., Moodus, Connecticut 06469. Perlene monofilament. Braided nylon and dacron lines. Fly lines.

Caravelle Boat Company, 2300 Redmond Road, Jacksonville, Arkansas 72076. Bass boats.

Carver Plastisols, Inc., P.O. Box 741, Minden, Louisiana 71055. Plastic, molds, materials, and equipment for making soft plastic lures. I've read that Carver formulates about 60 percent of the plastic used to manufacture soft plastic lures in the United States.

Cassville Distributing Company, 204 South Main Street, Cassville, Missouri 65625. This firm markets the Moon Glo Bass Lite, which casts a soft, wide beam for night fishing.

Challenger Boats, 3310 Hi-Lo Circle N.E., Huntsville, Alabama 35810. Challenger bass boats.

Lew Childre & Son, Inc., P.O. Box 535, Foley, Alabama 36535. The famous Lew's Speed Stick rods. Fuji guides and tips. Rod handles and reel seats. Power handles and high-speed gears for baitcasting reels. Childre also distributes a Japanese-made tapered monofilament line, and has recently added a baitcasting reel to their line.

Chrysler Marine Products, P.O. Box 2641, Detroit, Michigan 48231. Chrysler offers a complete line of outboards, from 150-horsepower "racing" motors on down to a 3.6 air-cooled kicker. They also offer electric-start motors on down to 10 horsepower. Chrysler makes a line of 15-, 16-, and 17-foot bass boats, which they call "multipurpose" fishing boats.

Cisco Kid Tackle, Inc., 2630 N.W. First Avenue, Boca Raton, Florida 33432. Cisco Kid lures, from top-water plugs to deep divers.

City Engineering Company, 3547 Massachusetts Avenue, Indianapolis, Indiana 46218. My-Te electric motors.

Dale Clemens Custom Tackle, Route 3, Box 415, Allentown, Pennsylvania 18104. Custom rods and rod-building tools and materials.

Clinton Engines Corporation, Maquoketa, Iowa 52060. Air-cooled outboards, from 3 to 9.9 horsepower.

Columbia Company, P.O. Box G, Columbia, Alabama 36319. Lures, including The Thing and The Bass Thing.

Cordell Tackle, Inc., P.O. Box 2020, Hot Springs, Arkansas 71901. Cordell is primarily a lure company, and they make the plastic Big-O, The Spot, Boy Howdy, and other bass catchers, including plastic worms and worming tackle. They also market a Lightnin' Rod series with walnut handles, along with high-speed gears, power casting handles, aluminum oxide guides, and a few other items of interest to bassmen.

Coren's Rod & Reel Service, 6619 North Clark Street, Chicago, Illinois 60626. In addition to reel and electric fishing motor repair, this firm stocks a wide selection of rod-building materials. They also market the Record 700 spinning reel, which is made in Switzerland. Catalog available.

Correct Craft, Inc., P.O. Box 13389, Orlando, Florida 32809. Bass boats.

Cortland Line Company, P.O. Box 1362, Cortland, New York 13045. This firm offers a variety of braided and monofilament fishing lines. Bassmen might be interested in their flat monofilament designed for baitcasting reels. Micro-Foam fly line. Micron braided line. Cortland now imports the Nylorfi monofilament, said to be France's most popular fishing line.

Creek Chub Bait Company, East Keyser Street, Garrett, Indiana 46738. Darter, Plunker, Jig-L-Worm, and other top-quality baits. The firm has sold over 40 million of their famous Pikie lures, and their jointed Wiggle-Fish caught the world's record bass (22 pounds 4 ounces) in 1932.

Creme Lure Company, P.O. Box 87, Tyler, Texas 75701. Nick Creme, a machinist from Akron, Ohio, made the first soft plastic worms in 1949. His firm now manufactures dozens of soft plastic baits, from his original Scoundrel worm down to mayfly nymphs. Although soft plastic baits are the mainstay of the firm's line, they also market worm hooks and sinkers, jigs, and a spinnerbait with four interchangeable blades.

J. Lee Cuddy Associates, 450 N.E. 79th Street, Miami, Florida 33138. This firm stocks a wide selection of blanks and rod-building materials, along with other items for fishermen.

Daiwa, 14011 South Normandie Avenue, Gardena, California 90249. This firm makes a wide selection of spinning and spincast reels. Their Millionaire V baitcasting reel was designed primarily for bass anglers, and the new model has a 5-to-1 retrieve ratio. Daiwa also makes fly reels and big game reels. Rods. Mono-Dex line.

Les Davis Fishing Tackle Company, 1565 Center Street, Tacoma, Washington 98409. Bolo spinners, spoons, Witch Doctor plugs, and other lures. Velus monofilament line.

Delhi Manufacturing Company, Illinois Avenue, Delhi, Louisiana 71232. Delhi makes the Terry line of bass boats, including the new

American Bass Fisherman high-performance job.

DeLong Lures, Inc., 85 Compark Road, Centerville, Ohio 45459. Although this firm makes a few jigs and spinnerbaits, soft plastic lures are their specialty. They make a 17-inch worm that is popular with some bassmen who go after lunkers only.

John Dory Boat Works, 14 West Meadow Lane, Stony Brook, New York 11790. Bass boats.

Dory U.S.A., Ltd., 1000 Jericho Turnpike, Huntington Station, New York 11746. Bass boats.

E. I. du Pont de Nemours & Company, Inc., 1007 Market Street, Wilmington, Delaware 19898. Stren monofilament.

DuraCraft Boats, Inc., Route 2, Monticello, Arkansas 71655. Bass boats.

Dura-Pak Corporation, P.O. Box 1173, Sioux City, Iowa 51102. Super Dude spinnerboats and other items for sportsmen.

Dutton-Lainson Company, P.O. Box 729, Hastings, Nebraska 68901. Electric anchor lifters; boat trailer accessories.

Dynaflex Manufacturing Corporation, 1075 West 21st Place, Hialeah, Florida 33010. Dynaflex rod blanks.

Ebbtide Corporation, Jones Creek Road, White Bluff, Tennessee 37187. Bass boats, featuring the 16-foot Bass Bandit.

Lou J. Eppinger Manufacturing Company, 6340 Schaefer Highway, Dearborn, Michigan 48126. Makers of the famous and widely imitated Dardevle spoons. The firm also makes a number of similar spoons and has recently introduced their Notangle Spinner, designed with a bent shaft to prevent line twist.

Eska Company, 2400 Kerper Boulevard, Dubuque, Iowa 52001. Outboards from 4.5 to 15 horsepower.

Evinrude Motors, P.O. Box 663, Milwaukee, Wisconsin 53201. Evinrude makes a complete line of outboards from 2 horsepower up to 135. They also make the Scout electric motors, available in either bow or stern mount, in 12-volt or 24-volt models. Evinrude also markets remote controls, instruments, marine batteries, and other boating accessories.

E-Z Company, 2908 East 15th Street, Tulsa, Oklahoma 74104. This firm makes the Lure Arranger tackle box, designed primarily for spinnerbaits.

Fabuglas Company, Inc., 6401 Centennial Boulevard, Nashville, Tennessee 37209. Bass boats, featuring the 16-foot Pro Fisherman with three live wells.

Falls Bait Company, Inc., 1440 Kennedy Road, Chippewa Falls, Wisconsin 54729. Miscellaneous lures.

Farenwald Enterprises, Inc., 330 Millwood Road, Lancaster, Pennsylvania 17602. Bass boats.

Featherweight Products, 3545–58 Ocean View Boulevard, Glendale, California 91208. Rawhide rod blanks; rod-building fittings and equipment. Hee-Haw lures. Rawhide monofilament line. Mono-Spooler, a gadget to help spool line on spinning and spincast reels.

Fenwick, P.O. Box 729, Westminster, California 92683. Fenwick makes a complete line of fiberglass and high-modulus graphite rods. Good stuff. They also publish an interesting newsletter at a subscription price of $1.00.

Feurer Brothers, Inc., 77 Lafayette Avenue, North White Plains, New York 10603. Bache Brown spinning reels. Other spinning, spincast, and fly reels.

Fiberking, Inc., P.O. Box 376, Smyrna, Tennessee 37167. Raider, Bassmaster, and Sportsman bass boats in deluxe and standard models.

Finnysports, 2910 Glanzman Road, Toledo, Ohio 43614. This firm publishes a large mail-order catalog featuring gear and materials for lure makers and rod builders. Also, name-brand lures, rods, reels, and other fishing gear.

Fireside Angler, Inc., P.O. Box 823, Melville, New York 11746. Fireside stocks a wide variety of tackle, and they have the largest selection of fishing books that I've seen in a catalog. Although they cater primarily to fly-rodders with such items as the expensive Walker reel, they also have a number of items of interest to bass anglers who use spinning or casting gear. Catalog available.

Fisher Marine, P.O. Box 1256, West Point, Mississippi 39773. Aluminum bass boats, canoes, and other boats. Their bass boats have a foam-lined inner decking that makes them much quieter than most aluminum boats.

Fishmaster Products, Inc., P.O. Box 9635, Tulsa, Oklahoma 74107. Fishmaster depth finders, Fishthometer temperature probe, and Depth-o-Lite underwater light meter. This firm also markets a wide-angle cylindrical transducer.

Fleck, 2728 7th Avenue S., Birmingham, Alabama 35233. Weed-Wader spinnerbaits.

Fo-Mac, Inc., 2621 North Iroquois Street, Tulsa, Oklahoma 47106. Surface temperature meters and other gear for bassmen and boaters.

G & R Industries, Inc., P.O. Box 18, Purdy, Missouri 65734. G & R's Silvertrol division makes electric motors, heavy-duty marine batteries, and battery chargers. They also market a neat T.E. (Total Electric) system for bass boats. Their Rogers lure division makes the Hawg Hunter, Craw-Pap, and other bass lures.

Gapen Tackle Company, Highway 10, Big Lake, Minnesota 55309. Fly rod lures, including the original Muddler Minnow. Keggo plastic worms and worming tackle. Jigs and jig spinners, such as the Hairy Worm Plus.

Garcia Corporation, 329 Alfred Avenue, Teaneck, New Jersey 07666. Garcia handles the famous Swedish-made Ambassadeur baitcasting reel, the French-made Mitchell spinning reels, and the Abu-Matic spincast reels. They have recently introduced a new family, the Kingfisher spinning and spincast reels. Also, Mitchell and Kingfisher fly reels. The firm offers a complete line of rods. Monofilament and braided lines, as well as fly lines. Dazzle Tail and other lures. Electro-Sonic depth finders and a new oxygen-temperature probe.

Gem Marine Products, P.O. Box 1408, Lake City, South Carolina 29560. This firm makes all sorts of brass and chrome-plated marine fittings, deck hardware, and so on, together with bilge pumps, remote controls, switches, lights. They also market a depth finder.

Generic Systems, Inc., P.O. Box 256, Rockaway, New Jersey 07886. This firm handles the French-made soft plastic Sosy Eel and Sosy Baitfish, both of which have amazingly realistic action.

Gentex Corporation, Carbondale, Pennsylvania 18407. Life jackets, boat seats, and other flotation devices made with Genucel, a permanently buoyant foam material that resists oil and gasoline.

Gladding-South Bend Tackle Company, Inc., South Otselic, New York 13155. Through its South Bend and Glen L. Evans divisions, Gladding offers a complete line of rods, spinning reels, lines, and lures, including the famous old Bass-Oreno wooden plug and the Shyster Spinner. The firm also makes the Aqua-Trol electric motors and the Bassin' Man depth finders (as well as the Aqua Search depth finders).

Glastex Company, 600 West 10th Avenue, Monmouth, Illinois 61462. Glastex manufactures a complete line of Sea Star runabout and family boats. Although their bass boats are limited to two models, The Hooker and The Catcher, they seem to be very well made. According to the firm, each Sea Star is 100 percent hand-laminated, has five stringers, and has all wooden parts completely sealed with resin.

Glastron Boat Company, P.O. Box 9447, Austin, Texas 78766. This firm makes the Beau Jack bass boats, together with a number of saltwater boats and family runabouts.

Goldline Corporation, 815 Enterprise Street, Cape Girardeau, Missouri 63701. Bass boats.

Grassl's Double 00, River Falls, Wisconsin 54022. Super Jig, Rasmatazz plastic worms and other lures, gadgets, and gear.

Greg Enterprises, P.O. Box 229, Fayetteville, Arkansas 72701. High-speed (4.8 to 1) conversion gears for the Ambassadeur and Million-aire reels. Also, a power handle with a nut retainer.

Grumman Boats, Grumman Allied Industries, Inc., Marathon, New York 13803. Well-made aluminum canoes and accessories.

Gudebrod Brothers Silk Company, Inc., 12 South 12th Street, Philadel-phia, Pennsylvania 19107. Dacron and nylon braided lines. Monofila-ment. Fly lines. Top-quality plugs. Rod-winding threads. Aetna guides.

Gull of Bristol, Inc., P.O. Box 204, North Dartmouth, Massachusetts 02747. Bass boats.

Harrison-Hoge Industries, Inc., 104 Arlington Avenue, St. James, New York 11780. Weed Wing, Panther Martin, and other lures.

Heath Company, Benton Harbor, Michigan 49022. Heath offers several electronic kits for do-it-yourself anglers. Depth finder kits are avail-able, including a digital readout unit. Heath also markets a "Thermo Spotter" temperature probe, a fuel vapor detector, and a power in-verter that converts the boat battery's 12-volt DC output to 117-volt AC, in case the bassman wants to take his electric razor or coffeepot along.

James Heddon's Sons, 414 West Street, Dowagiac, Michigan 49047. In 1897, James Heddon whittled the world's first wooden plug. Since then, the firm has manufactured some classic bass catchers, such as the Lucky 13, the Zara Spook, and the River Runt. In addition to their line of lures, the firm also manufactures baitcasting, spinning, spincast, and fly reels. They have a complete line of rods, some of which are fitted with the new Sintox aluminum oxide guides and tips.

Helin Tackle Company, 4099 Beaufait Street, Detroit, Michigan 48207. Flatfish and other lures.

Herter's, Route 1, Waseca, Minnesota 56093. Everything. Send $1.00 for their huge catalog.

John J. Hildebrandt Corporation, P.O. Box 50, Logansport, Indiana 46947. Spinnerbaits, spoons, and other lures. Spinner blades, jig spin-ners, and plastic skirts.

E. Hille, P.O. Box 269, Williamsport, Pennsylvania 17701. Materials and tools for rod building, fly tying, and lure making. Tackle boxes, fishing tubes, and so on. Catalog available; mail orders welcome.

Hofschneider Corporation, P.O. Box 4166, Rochester, New York 14611. Red Eye spoons and spinners.

Honda Motor Company, 100 West Alondra Boulevard, Gardena, California 90247. Honda makes a small outboard motor (7.5 horsepower) that uses a pressure-fed lubricating system, which eliminates the need for premixing oil and gasoline.

Hopkins Lure Company, 1130 Boissevain Avenue, Norfolk, Virginia 23507. Hopkins makes a line of spoons, and many bassmen like them for yo-yoing.

Hosea Manufacturing Company, P.O. Box 609, Quitman, Texas 75783. Bass boats, featuring the Renegade 16, which has a "tunnel hull" design that is said to be safer in rough water.

Hydra-Sports, 13th and G Streets, Smyrna, Tennessee 37167. This firm makes the sleek Hydra-Sports high-performance boats, available in several models and lengths.

Industrial Plastics of Louisburg, Inc., P.O. Box 672, Wake Forest, North Carolina 27587. Mackie 16-foot bass boats.

Invader Corporation, P.O. Box 238, Giddings, Texas 78942. Bass boats.

Ray Jefferson, Main and Cotton Streets, Philadelphia, Pennylvania 19127. This leading manufacturer of marine electronic equipment markets a complete line of depth finders for bass anglers. They also market the Sentry oxygen monitor, which was first sold through a Texas firm called Bass-Ox. The Ray Jefferson line also includes Citizens Band radios, radio direction finders, and expensive battery chargers.

Jetco Electronics, Inc., 1133 Barranca Street, El Paso, Texas 79935. Sea Scope depth finders and Electra Pal electric motors.

Johnny Reb Lure Company, P.O. Box 902, Clinton, Mississippi 39056. In addition to bass lures, Johnny Reb makes the original "Norton" anchor, which is vinyl-coated. They also make the LectrAnchor system, used on boats in the Bassmaster's Classic tournament. They have recently introduced a spring-loaded stump-jumper device for bow-mounted electric motors.

Louis Johnson Company, 1547 Old Deerfield Road, Highland Park, Illinois 60035. This firm makes the famous Johnson Silver Minnow and other spoons. They also market a 44-inch Brush Rod.

Johnson Outboards, 200 Sea-Horse Drive, Waukegan, Illinois 60085. A division of Outboard Marine Corporation, Johnson offers a complete line of outboards, from 2 horsepower to 135. They also market two electric motors, one a foot-controlled bow-mount unit and the other a transom mount. Both are available in either 12- or 24-volt models.

Johnson Reels Company, 1531 Madison Avenue, Mankato, Minnesota 56001. Sabra, Citation, and other spincast reels. Apparently Lloyd Johnson invented the closed-face spincast reels.

K-Mac & Company, P.O. Box 303, Addison, Texas 75001. Bass Buddy Mini-Boat, a plastic "innertube" with built-in molded seat and contour backrest. The firm also markets latex waders and other items for sportsmen, including an electronic mosquito repeller.

Knight Manufacturing Company, Inc., P.O. Box 3162, Tyler, Texas 75701. Bass Cracker and other lures.

Kodiak Corporation, P.O. Box 467, Ironwood, Michigan 49938. A complete line of fiberglass fishing rods.

L & S Bait Company, Inc., 1500 East Bay Drive, Largo, Florida 33540. Mirrolure plugs in 67 models, from top-water to superdeep runners.

Lazy Ike Corporation, P.O. Box 1177, Fort Dodge, Iowa 50501. This firm makes the famous Lazy Ike banana plugs, together with miscellaneous baits.

H. L. Leonard Rod Company, 25 Cottage Street, Midland Park, New Jersey 07432. The spirit of this firm is captured, I think, by the slogan on their letterhead: "Manufacturers of rather fine fishing rods and tackle since 1869." They do make "rather fine" bamboo, fiberglass, and graphite rods, and their mail-order department markets the Pescador spinning reels and Hardy fly reels, as well as various lures and lines. Their large fly selection includes bass bugs. They also market miscellaneous fishing gear and outdoor attire. Catalog available.

Limit Manufacturing Corporation, P.O. Box 369, Richardson, Texas 75080. Materials and equipment for making plastic worms, jigs, and rods. Retails name-brand lures and other products. Mail-order catalog available.

Linden Manufacturing Company, Inc., P.O. Box 930, Linden, Texas 75563. This firm makes the Caddo tri-hull bass boat and a semi-vee model with a pedestal fishing seat up front. At the time of this writing, Linden has a new Deluxe Bass Pro in the making. It will be a combination ski and fishing boat, with removable seats and various seating possibilities.

Lindy, P.O. Box 488, Brainerd, Minnesota 56410. Spinnerbaits, jigs, plastic worms, and other lures. Terminal tackle, including the famous Lindy Rigs for bait fishing. Transducer mounts, including

the Mini-Bracket that fits on the shaft of an electric motor and including fold-back front deck and fold-up transom mounts.

Little Beaver Manufacturing Company, 1244 Lafayette Avenue, Terre
Haute, Indiana 47804. Rattler capsules for plastic worms and other
lures. Stop It quick-kill devices for bass boats.

Lowrance Electronics, Inc., 12000 East Skelly Drive, Tulsa, Oklahoma
74128. Originators of the famous Fish Lo-K-Tor, Lowrance now
makes a number of top-notch depth finders, as well as an electronic
temperature probe and surface temperature meter. Fish-N-Float
buoy marker kits.

Lund American, Inc., P.O. Box 10, New York Mills, Minnesota 56567.
Lund makes a line of aluminum and fiberglass boats, but they don't
offer much of a choice in bass boats. In fact, what they call a bass
boat is really a semi-vee with slat seats. Their "guide boat," however,
is pretty close to a bass boat except that the bow deck is sunken,
which would cause problems in mounting an electric motor.

Mann's Bait Company, P.O. Box 604, Eufaula, Alabama 36207. Little
George tail spinner, Jelly Worms, and other lures.

Marathon Tackle, Route 2, Mosinee, Wisconsin 54455. Spoons, spinners,
and bass bugs.

Marine Metal Products Company, 1222 Range Avenue, Clearwater,
Florida 33515. Bait Saver and Super Saver live well and bait bucket
aerators. The Super Saver oxygenates live well water to within 0.4
percent of the maximum amount of oxygen dissolvable in water at
71 degrees F. The firm also makes various marine accessories.

Martin Lizzard Manufacturing Company, 1850 East Troy Avenue, Indianapolis, Indiana 46203. This firm makes a large deep-diving plug
similar to the Hellbender.

Martin Reel Company, Inc., P.O. Drawer 8, Mohawk, New York 13407.
Wide selection of fly rods and reels. Martin made the first automatic
fly reel back in 1884. They have a limited line of tackle boxes, lines,
and lures. Spinning and spincast reels, including the French-made
Martin Bretton. Fiberglass fishing rods.

Mason Tackle Company, Otisville, Michigan 48463. If my information
is correct, Mason Tackle Company invented monofilament fishing
line. They now market the Bass-On and other monofilaments as well
as braided nylon and dacron.

Master Molders, Inc., P.O. Box 815, Clarksville, Texas 75426. Several
models of KingFisher fiberglass bass boats. These boats have a reputation for toughness and are 100 percent hand laminated.

Maxwell Manufacturing Company, P.O. Box 649, Vancouver, Washington 98660. Lures, spinners, terminal tackle, landing nets, etc. Handmade Grizzly rods.

McCollum's Lunker Bass Lures, 611 19th Street, Tuscaloosa, Alabama 35401. This firm specializes in spinnerbaits, and their Bush Hog was apparently the first spinnerbait with a long "snag guard" arm. At present, their line also includes the Brush Hog and Top Hog. The latter is a spinnerbait designed especially for buzzing. Some models have a snap to facilitate changing blades.

Mercer Fishing Tackle Company, Inc., P.O. Box 5413, Lawton, Oklahoma 73501. Laddie lures.

Mercury Marine, 1939 Pioneer Road, Fond du Lac, Wisconsin 54935. Mercury outboards and Mercruiser inboard/outboard motors. Quicksilver remote controls, power trim, and other accessories. Also, Mercury has recently introduced an electric motor to their line.

Midland Tackle Company, 66 Route 17, Sloatsburg, New York 10974. Tools and material for lure makers and rod builders. Miscellaneous fishing items, such as "pearl" spinner blades made from natural shell.

Mildrum Manufacturing Company, 230 Berlin Street, East Berlin, Connecticut 06023. Rod guides and tips.

Mille Lacs Manufacturing Company, P.O. Box 27, Isle, Minnesota 56342. Little Joe fishing tackle, including jigs, spinner blades, jig spinners, and miscellaneous lures.

3M Company, 3M Center, St. Paul, Minnesota 55101. Phillipson rods.

Minn-Kota Manufacturing Company, 201 North 17th Street, Moorhead, Minnesota 56560. Believe it or not, this firm has been manufacturing electric fishing motors since 1932. They now have 11 models in their line, including foot-controlled units and 24-volt models. They also make 3 air-cooled models, and, since the motors are out of the water, they don't produce as much drag as water-cooled models.

Bruce B. Mises, Inc., 1122 South Robertson Boulevard, Los Angeles, California 90035. This firm is the American distributor of Maxima monofilament, made in West Germany. They also market a new Mono-Slik device that cleans and lubricates monofilament and braided line. It fits over the line (just above the last rod guide) and coats it with a silicone lubricant during the retrieve.

Mister Twister, Inc., P.O. Box 598, Minden, Louisiana 71055. Makers of the suddenly famous Mister Twister soft plastic lures. Now available in a dozen sizes and designs. The firm also markets Mister Twisters rigged on jigs and spinnerbaits.

MonArk Boat Company, P.O. Box 210, Monticello, Arkansas 71655. Fiberglass bass boats, from the 14-foot Delta I to the 18-foot Marauder inboard/outboard. MonArk also makes a complete line of aluminum fishing boats, including 14- and 16-foot Bass Special models with upright foam flotation.

Montgomery Ward, 618 West Chicago Avenue, Chicago, Illinois 60607. Sea King electric and outboard motors.

Motor-Guide, P.O. Box 551, Starkville, Mississippi 39759. A division of Herschede Hall Clock Company, this firm makes the Motor-Guide permanent magnet electric motors. The 24-volt Magnum Motor-Guide is their newest model. The firm also markets a neat electric anchor lifter.

O. Mustad & Son, Inc., P.O. Box 838, Auburn, New York 13021. Fish hooks. Established in 1832, Mustad now markets hooks in over 130 countries. Anyone interested in hooks should get a copy of their 45-page catalog.

National Expert, Inc., 2928 Stevens Avenue South, Minneapolis, Minnesota 55408. Vibro-Tail soft plastic lures, spoons, and other baits.

Nelson-Dykes Company, Inc., 4071 Shilling Way, Dallas, Texas 75237. "Dilly" boat trailers. Their Drive-On 1400 was made especially for bass boats.

Netcraft Company, 3101 Sylvania Street, Toledo, Ohio 43613. This mail-order firm publishes a 170-odd-page catalog of rods, reels, lures, terminal tackle, materials for do-it-yourselfers, and netting. Odds and ends.

Newland Lure Company, P.O. Box 266, Bull Shoals, Arkansas 72619. Various spinnerbaits, jigs, and other lures. Some of their spinnerbaits have nylon weed guards, and their Buzzin Cuzzin model has a snap to facilitate changing spinner blades.

Newton Line Company, Inc., Homer, New York 13077. Fishing lines.

Norman Manufacturing Company, Inc., 2910 Jenny Lind Road, Fort Smith, Arkansas 72901. Rat-Lur, Big-N, Spino-Spider, and other bass lures. Ranger plastic worms, which have a cone-shaped tail with twice the buoyancy of regular worm tails.

Normark Corporation, 1710 East 78th Street, Minneapolis, Minnesota 55423. Rapala lures, made in Finland. Rapala fillet knives. In addition to the original balsa Rapala, the firm now offers several hardwood lures, such as the Rapala Magnum and the Deep-Diver.

Okiebug Distributing Company, 3501 South Sheridan Street, Tulsa, Oklahoma 74145. Okiebug has a large catalog exclusively for bass anglers, and mail orders are welcome. The firm carries a very large stock of lures and other bass tackle, and they also manufacture their own line of spinnerbaits—the Okiebugs.

Old Town Canoe Company, Old Town, Maine 04468. Canoes, including some made from Kevlar, a new flame-resistant material developed by du Pont. Kevlar is 40 percent lighter than fiberglass.

OMC Parts and Accessories, Outboard Marine Corporation, Galesburg, Illinois 61401. Parts and accessories for Johnson and Evinrude motors. Boating accessories.

The Orvis Company, Inc., Manchester, Vermont 05254. Although Orvis caters primarily to fly-fishermen, they do offer a lot of interesting gear for bass anglers who use spinning or baitcasting rigs. In addition to fine bamboo, fiberglass, and graphite fly rods, they offer a family of spinning reels and spinning rods. No push-button stuff. Bass bugs and flies and complete fly-tying materials. Fancy attire and miscellaneous items, such as watertight camera bags.

Ouachita Marine and Industrial Corporation, 721 Main Street, Little Rock, Arkansas 72201. Ouchita makes several bass boats in its Convincer series. Their new Advancer boats are big and heavy enough for coastal waters, but they are basically bass boats. The firm also makes aluminum boats and canoes, and their aluminum bass boats (B Boats) come in 14-, 15-, 16-, 18-, and 20-foot lengths.

Padre Island Company, 2617 North Zarzamora Street, San Antonio, Texas 78201. Miscellaneous lures.

P.C. Fishing Tackle, Inc., 720 West Second Street, Owensboro, Kentucky 42301. Bluper, Lott-A-Leech, and other bass lures.

E. H. Peckinpaugh Company, P.O. Box 15044, Baton Rouge, Louisiana 70815. Bass bugs, Peck's weighted casting flies, and other lures. Founded in 1910, this firm offers the oldest line of popping bugs on the market; in fact, the cork popping bug is said to have been invented by E. H. Peckinpaugh.

Penn Fishing Tackle Manufacturing Company, 3028 West Hunting Park Avenue, Philadelphia, Pennsylvania 19132. Levelmatic baitcasting reels and Spinfisher spinning reels. Penn also makes a number of reels for big game fishing.

Pflueger Sporting Goods Division, P.O. Box 310, Hallandale, Florida 33009. Pflueger has been making fishing tackle for 110 years. Supreme, Akron, and other baitcasting reels; Skilcast and other spincast reels. International spinning reels. Fly reels. A complete line of rods. Braided, monofilament, and fly lines. Miscellaneous lures. Pflueger offers a line of permanent magnet electric motors, including a dandy new 24-volt model. They also market a remote-control attachment that can be used with transom-mount electrics.

Phillips Fly & Tackle Company, P.O. Box 188, Alexandria, Pennsylvania 16611. Crippled Killer top-water lures, bass bugs, and flies.

Plano Molding Company, Plano, Illinois 60545. This firm offers a large selection of plastic tackle boxes. Their new 6500 box was designed to hold both plastic worms and spinnerbaits, together with other lures.

Polar Kraft Manufacturing Company, P.O. Box 708, Olive Branch, Mississippi 38654. Aluminum bass boats, including 14-, 15-, and 16-foot Bass Fisherman models with pedestal easy seats and other bass boat features.

Eddie Pope & Company, 25572 Stanford Avenue, Valencia, California 91355. Lures, worming tackle, and fishing accessories.

Power Cat of Texas, 3206 Coffey Street, Victoria, Texas 77901. This firm offers several models of Power Cat hand-laminated bass boats.

Powerwinch, 184 Garden Street, Bridgeport, Connecticut 06605. This firm makes electric winches and hoists for trailers and boat houses. They now have an electric anchor windlass, which is available for either 12- or 24-volt electrical systems.

Prescott Spinner Company, 1000 Fairview Avenue, Hamilton, Ohio 45015. Paul Bunyans and other spinners. Spoons. Jig spinners in various colors and styles. Prescott is now a division of Fred Arbogast Company.

Quick Corporation of America, 620 Terminal Way, Costa Mesa, California 92627. Spinning reels, Finessa rods, Damyl monofilament. Quick has recently added a baitcasting reel to their line.

Quick Draw Sporting Goods Company, P.O. Box 333, Richardson, Texas 75080. Custom-tailored rod holders molded to hold Ambassadeur reels.

Rabble Rouser Lures, 500 South 7th Street, Fort Smith, Arkansas 72901. Several rattler lures, including the Di-Dapper crankbait, the Rouster, and the Rabble Rouser Topwater. Yum Yum worms.

Ram-Glas Products, Inc., 618 East Markham Street, Little Rock, Arkansas 72201. Electric fishing motors, boat reins, and electric anchor systems.

Rangeley Region Sports Shop, 28 Main Street, Rangeley, Maine 04970. Mail order, more or less specializing in fly fishing tackle and gear.

Ranger Boats, Wood Manufacturing Company, Inc., Flippin, Arkansas

72634. Founded only a few years ago by a professional bass guide, this firm quickly became one of the leaders of bass boat manufacture. They offer a complete line of bass boats, including a couple of inboard/outboards and high-performance models.

Ranger Tackle Company, Inc., P.O. Box 6383, Fort Smith, Arkansas 72901. Threadfin-Shad, spoons, and other lures.

Rebel, P.O. Box 1587, Fort Smith, Arkansas 72901. Rebel offers several models of bass boats, including two with inboard/outboard engines. They also market color-coordinated trailers that were designed especially for Rebel bass boat hulls. Electric motors. Rocket Shad, Rebel Minnow, Destroyer spinnerbaits, and other lures.

Reb Manufacturing Company, 549 North Saginaw Street, Pontiac, Michigan 48058. Rods. Bayou-Special spoons.

Recreational Development, Inc., P.O. Box 4029, Tallahassee, Florida 32303. Diamond Rattler lures and Rattleworm, a slip sinker with sound chamber designed for use with plastic worms.

Reed Tackle, P.O. Box 390, Caldwell, New Jersey 07006. Reed-Flex tubular fiberglass rod blanks and Champion rod handles. Rod-building fittings. Jig heads, spinner blades, and lure-making parts. A complete line of fly-tying tools and materials. Reed publishes a large catalog and welcomes mail orders.

Reel Power Equipment, Inc., 811 42nd Street South, St. Petersburg, Florida 33711. Electric anchor lifts.

Rhyan-Craft Boat Manufacturing Company, 1700 South Jackson Road, El Dorado, Arkansas 71730. Bass boats.

Richland Manufacturing Company, Route 1, Lebanon, Missouri 65536. Bass boats.

Ric-Jig Tackle, Inc., Island View Route, International Falls, Minnesota 56649. Jigs, spinnerbaits, plastic worms. Their CyCo Worm Spin spinnerbaits are unique in that they have Texas-rig worm hooks attached to them.

St. Croix Corporation, 9909 South Shore Drive, Minneapolis, Minnesota 55441. St. Croix makes a complete line of rods, including the Stud Stix series with Fuji guides and tips. Their Compac division makes spinning, spincast, and fly reels, along with hooks, lures, and other tackle.

Scientific Anglers, Inc., P.O. Box 2001, Midland, Michigan 48640. Air Cel and Wet Cel fly lines. Expensive fiberglass fly rods and matching reels. Their reels are made by Hardy Brothers in England. The importance of balance of rod, reel, and line is the whole idea behind Scientific Anglers.

Sears, Roebuck and Company, Sears Tower, Chicago, Illinois 60684. Sears markets a complete line of fishing and boating gear, including a budget bass boat. Their Ted Williams line includes rods, reels, depth finders, and so on. Most of the retail stores don't stock all this stuff, and it is not all listed in their general catalogs. Write for a copy of their Boating and Fishing Catalog.

Shakespeare Fishing Tackle Division, 241 East Kalamazoo Avenue, Kalamazoo, Michigan 49001. This giant of the tackle industry introduced the first fiberglass rods shortly after World War II. They now offer a complete line of rods, including a graphite fly rod. They also make a number of spinning, spincast, and baitcasting reels, including a "total free spooling" fast-retrieve model with big handles. The firm has a wide selection of monofilament, braided nylon, and dacron line.

In the electronics department, Shakespeare makes three models of ScanMaster depth finders and several models of their WonderTroll electric motors. They also market a WonderGuide remote-control unit for electric motors that were made without a foot-control mechanism.

Shakespeare makes a number of plugs in their Paw Paw line, and some of these are made of wood instead of plastic. Old-timers (and others) who lament the passing of wooden plugs should write for a catalog.

Shannon Lure Company, 3654 West Montrose Avenue, Chicago, Illinois 60618. Bass Bandit and other spinnerbaits. Shannon Twin Spinner bucktail was one of the original lures with top-riding spinners.

Sheldon's, Inc., P.O. Box 1001, Antigo, Wisconsin 54409. The world-famous Mepps spinners, Kriss spoons, and bucktails.

Skeeter Products, P.O. Box 1602, Kilgore, Texas 75662. Hawk Pro, Super Skeeter, and other bass boats. Custom interior available; write for details. This firm was instrumental in the early development of bass boats.

Jack K. Smithwick & Son, P.O. Box 1205, Shreveport, Louisiana 71163. Devil's Horse, Water Gator, and other lures.

Snagproof, 4153 East Galbraith Road, Cincinnati, Ohio 45236. Weedless frogs and other lures.

Southeastern Marine Supply, Inc., P.O. Box 4458, Huntsville, Alabama

35802. Hawkeye depth finders, E-Z Trim, various mounts for depth finders, electric motors, anchors, and fishing seats. Boat trailers.

Sportscraft, Inc., P.O. Box 8217, Houston, Texas, 77004. Water-ator bait wells and aerators for live wells.

Sportsman's Products, Inc., P.O. Box 37, Marion, Indiana 46952. This firm makes a variety of plastic worms and worm rigs. Min-O-Spin lures and spinnerbaits.

Starcraft Boats, 2703 College Avenue, Goshen, Indiana 46526. Bass boats, featuring the Pro 18. The new Bassmaster 16 design allows the customer to help outfit his own boat.

Stearns Manufacturing Company, P.O. Box 1498, St. Cloud, Minnesota 56301. Stearns manufactures a complete line of sharp-looking life jackets and vests. Anglers who fish for bass on remote ponds and small streams might consider their Sportsvest Sans-Souci, which is made primarily for hunters. Stearns uses Aquafoam flotation material, which is a closed-cell polyvinyl chloride foam that can't waterlog and never loses buoyancy.

Stembridge Products, Inc., P.O. Box 90756, East Point, Georgia 30344. Fliptail soft plastic lures and worm-fishing gear. The firm has recently introduced the first C.R.T. sonar unit for bass anglers.

Stemco Manufacturing Company, P.O. Box 1205, Longview, Texas 75601. Bass boats.

Steury Corporation, 310 Steury Avenue, Goshen, Indiana 46526. This firm makes a wide variety of family boats and larger craft for pleasure and saltwater fishing. They also make 15- and 16-foot bass boats.

Storm Manufacturing Company, P.O. Box 265, Norman, Oklahoma 73069. ThinFin shad-shaped plugs, Fats-O, Bass Hog spinnerbaits, and other lures.

Strike King Lure Company, Inc., 2805 Sanderwood Street, Memphis, Tennessee 38118. Happy Hooker tailspinners, Spense Scout, Spense Spook, Big S, spinnerbaits, and soft plastic lures.

Stryker Boats, 5010 Beechmont Drive, N.E., Huntsville, Alabama 35811. Stryker features 15- and 17-foot high-performance bass boats.

Stump Knocker Boats, P.O. Box 26, Headland, Alabama 36345. This small firm makes the Stump Knocker, a one-man craft designed for bass fishing in creeks and small ponds.

Sunset Line & Twine Company, Jefferson and Erwin Streets, Petaluma, California 94952. Monofilament and braided lines. Masterline imported fly lines.

nerbaits, jigs, soft plastic lures, jig spinners. The founder of this firm designed the widely imitated Pony Head jig.

Winner Boats, P.O. Box 667, Dickson, Tennessee 37055. Bass boats.

Wonder State Trailer Company, Inc., 124, Industrial Drive, Jacksonville, Arkansas 72076. Boat trailers, featuring the Custom Bass boat trailer.

Woodstream Corporation, P.O. Box 327, Lititz, Pennsylvania 17543. Hydron scented lures, Old Pal tackle boxes, spinning and spincast reels, and rods.

The Worth Company, P.O. Box 88, Stevens Point, Wisconsin 54481. Fishing lures and accessories. Anchormate anchor control.

Wright & McGill Company, 4245 East 46th Avenue, Denver, Colorado 80216. This firm makes the famous Eagle Claw tackle and hooks. They offer a wide selection of rods and several models of spinning, spincast, and fly reels. Blond monofilament.

Yakima Bait Company, P.O. Box 310, Granger, Washington 98932. Rooster Tail and other lures. Monofilament line.

Zebco, P.O. Box 270, Tulsa, Oklahoma 74101. Although Zebco is famous for its spincast push-button reels, the firm also markets a complete line of open-faced spinning reels, including the Cardinal series. Zebco also makes the Pro Staff rods. Spinnerbaits and other lures, including the famous Doll Fly jigs.

Zorro Bait Company, 1315 51st Avenue North, Nashville, Tennessee 37209. Aggravator spinnerbaits, Flappin-Shad, and soft plastic worms. Zorro also makes a power handle for baitcasting reels.

Index